THE ENCHANTED ASTROLOGER

YOUR PERSONAL ORACLE

Monte Farber & Amy Zerner

THOMAS DUNNE BOOKS
ST. MARTIN'S PRESS ⚯ NEW YORK

DEDICATION

The Enchanted Astrologer is dedicated to the
inspiring memory of Jessie Spicer Zerner, Ma,
the most wonderful mother, friend, and
co-worker possible; and to Kit-Kat,
our gorgeous little calico muse. May the love
we all shared continue to enchant our
lives until we meet again.

THE ENCHANTED ASTROLOGER

YOUR PERSONAL ORACLE

Monte Farber & Amy Zerner

For information, address St. Martin'sPress, 175 Fifth Avenue,
New York, N.Y. 10010

Library of Congress Cataloging-in-Publication Data
available on request.

ISBN: 0-312-25173-4

Thomas Dunne Books
An imprint of St. Martin's Press

First U.S. Edition published in 2001

10 9 8 7 6 5 4 3 2 1

Printed in China through Colorcraft Ltd., Hong Kong

Design and Production:
Rose Sheifer - Graphic Productions
Walnut Creek, California

Zerner/Farber Editions, Ltd.
Box 2299
East Hampton, NY 11937
E-mail: info@TheEnchantedWorld.com
Website: www.TheEnchantedWorld.com

INDEX

THE SIGNS OF THE ZODIAC

THE PLANETS OF ASTROLOGY

P
L
A
N
E
T
S

P
L
A
N
E
T
S

THE HOUSES OF A HOROSCOPE

H
O
U
S
E
S

INTRODUCTION

*T*he word *enchant* is derived from and means the same thing as the Latin word incantare, to sing or chant into (in meaning "in" and cantare for "to sing" or "to chant"). What a wonderful way to describe the feeling we get when something enchants us! It is as if a song has been sung or chanted right into us, a magical song that has gone straight to our hearts and cast its delightfully charming spell. It is no wonder that tales of enchantment are always the most popular stories with children, children of all ages and Ages.

The word astrology has an equally beautiful origin. It is derived from the combination of the ancient Greek words astron, meaning "star," and logos meaning "logic." Star-logic!

We have named this oracle *The Enchanted Astrologer* because it is a way of tapping into the magic that astrology has to offer, instantly. It is designed to enchant you with the logic of the stars. To do this, we have used the rich symbolic language of the Planets, Signs, and Houses of astrology to offer you guidance. You can use *The Enchanted Astrologer* to answer your questions about Love/Relationships, Work/Career, and Wealth/Success. You can also use it to learn a lot about your astrology sign and those of your family and friends. It can help you to understand individual character traits and the many challenging issues we all face in life, and it will also help you to deal with them successfully. It does this by helping you to make better decisions. The best part is that you can use it now, without your having to spend decades researching and studying astrology, because we have distilled the essence of this ancient art into a system that can answer your most important questions.

The Planets of astrology symbolize the various aspects of our personality that move us to take various actions. The word "planet" itself is taken from the Greek word for "wanderer" because, to ancient observers, planets seemed to be stars that moved through the heavens against the background of the signs of the Zodiac.

The word "zodiac" is taken from yet another Greek word meaning "circle of animals," in the manner of a circus parade. This is the way the Signs of the Zodiac are derived from the constellations, symbolized mainly by animal forms, which occupy the band of outer space surrounding the Earth's equator. The planets move through the signs of the zodiac. When they are passing through a sign, each planet is said to be "in" the sign it is passing through. Each of the signs represents a different way to approach the world. In astrology, the sign a planet is passing through modifies and blends its meaning with the energies signified by that planet.

Most people are familiar with their astrological sign, which is based on the date of their birth. If you are not, then look up your sign in the Index on pages 6 & 7. A person's Sun sign is the sign of the zodiac that the Sun appeared to be in, as viewed from Earth, at the moment of her or his birth. We can learn a lot about ourselves and others just from knowing where the Sun was when they were born. However, the total power of astrology is made available to us when we use our personal horoscope (from the Greek horo for "hour" and skopos meaning "to look at"), the map of how the planets lined up around us at the moment of our birth.

If you look at a horoscope, it looks like a pizza pie with twelve slices. *

Each "slice" literally symbolizes a slice of life, the areas of our everyday life in which the energies of the various planets will manifest, qualified by the signs they are in. The Houses of an astrological horoscope chart wheel are where the planets "dwell." Knowing where they are in a person's chart can tell you about their personality, the cycles of their life, and even describe and predict tendencies in their past, present, and future that can result in various

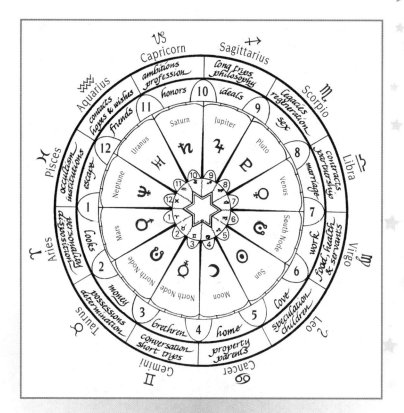

events and actions. There is an old saying, "Your character is your destiny." This has certainly been true for me.

My name is Monte Farber and I live a life that, to most people, seems enchanted. Since 1974, I have been with my wife and soul mate, Amy Zerner, building a loving partnership unlike any other marriage we have ever seen or even heard about. Our highly successful relationship as lovers, creative collaborators, and business partners is partially a result of a practical application of the ancient wisdom we both studied before and during our marriage—wisdom we have made available to everyone in each of our divination systems and CD-ROMs such as "The Enchanted Tarot," "The Alchemist," "The Instant Tarot Reader," "The Oracle of The Goddess," "Karma Cards," "The Psychic Circle," "The Pathfinder Psychic Talking Board," and "Gifts of The Goddess" affirmation cards.

Until I met Amy, I had thought that astrology was a bunch of nonsense. However, she was studying astrology and I was studying Amy. Since I respected her, I kept my mind open to what she respected. I'm glad I did. After I studied it a bit, I was amazed to realize that astrology was really a powerful language of psychology, personality, and character — a language with the power to help me change my life for the better.

Amy and I do not just create our divination systems — we use them all the time to help us make better decisions. Like most of you, we have a lot of decisions to make. We could not have done all of our books and Amy could not have created her more than six hundred incredibly beautiful National Endowment for the Arts award-winning fabric collage tapestries without them. Through our work together, we have helped people around the globe to make their inner world a more beautiful and empowering place so that they are better equipped to deal with the frenzied pace of modern life.

Since childhood, I have truly believed that the purpose of life is to be happy. Yet, like everyone, throughout my life I have sometimes found myself not feeling happy at all. On one of those days I asked Amy "What do you think is the common denominator of all human-caused suffering?" Without a moment's hesitation she replied, "Poor decision-making."

It is hard for most people to admit their mistakes. It is painful to admit even to ourselves that we could have and should have been able to foresee the outcome of our decisions and the actions we took based on those decisions. However, deep down inside, it is hard for anyone to deny that it has usually been his or her own poor decisions that have led to their difficulties. We grow by learning from these lessons, but we can also grow by getting to know ourselves better and learning how to make better decisions. That is what The Enchanted Astrologer is designed for.

Of course there are those who are challenged by the circumstances of their birth or by accidents. However, as the inspirational stories of Helen Keller and many other people have shown, when we are challenged by circumstances over which we have no apparent control, we still have the power to decide how we are going to react to those circumstances. Are we going spend our time bemoaning our fate or are we going to experience the hard times, pick ourselves up, learn from our situation as best we can, and do the best we can?

Like astrology itself, *The Enchanted Astrologer* is a complete system designed to help you understand yourself better so that you can make better decisions. It is not designed to make the decisions for you. There are visualization techniques in this book that are going to help you put yourself into the state of relaxed concentration necessary for learning and good decision-making to take place. When you are in a state of relaxed concentration, you will best be able to make use of the advice contained in this book. Everything we have put into *The Enchanted Astrologer* comes from our experience as astrologers and as counselors, artists, friends, family members, business people, and soul mates.

Unlike most books, *The Enchanted Astrologer* is all about you; it is a complete system designed to help you take action to make your life better. How much better can you make your life? That is a combination of your present circumstances and how much effort you are willing to give to make your life better. Don't get me wrong, using *The Enchanted Astrologer* is not difficult and it's not work — it's fun, pure and simple. But like all fun, it has a purpose. And like all things with a purpose, it requires awareness of your purpose and dedication to your purpose to reach your goals. It is designed to help you remember that you can make your life better and to help you do it. It can help you remember that right now and in this very moment that only you have the ability to make the decisions that govern your actions.

Your actions got you where you are now. If you had the power to get yourself where you are now, you also have the power to get yourself to where you want to be. Only you have the power to improve your life and The Enchanted Astrologer can help you do it while you are having fun and learning about yourself and about astrology, too.

How to use The Enchanted Astrologer

Using The Enchanted Astrologer to answer your questions about Love/Relationships, Work/Career, or Wealth/Success is as easy as shuffling the deck of thirty-six Planet, Sign, and House cards, choosing one of them, and then looking up the meaning of the card you picked in this book.

In this book's index you will find the page number for that card's meaning in answer to the type of question you asked, either about Love/Relationships, Work/Career, or Wealth/Success. Your question will be answered with advice based on the ancient meanings of the Planet, House, or Sign of the Zodiac that you picked, updated and interpreted for our modern age.

You do not have to have any prior knowledge of astrology and there is never anything that you have to memorize. However, after using The Enchanted Astrologer by yourself and with your friends and family, you may be surprised to realize that you are starting to be quite familiar with the meanings of the Signs of the zodiac, the Planets of astrology, and the meanings of the Houses of a personal horoscope chart. Astrology is a language that is fairly easy to learn and once you learn it, you can gain fascinating insights into yourself, your partner, your friends, your family, and anyone whose astrology chart you can obtain.

How to ask your question

The Enchanted Astrologer is designed to answer your questions about Love/Relationships, Work/Career, or Wealth/Success. To obtain your answer, you should phrase your question in either the following master form or by using one of its variations listed below:

"Tell me what I need to know now about
    (Love/Relationships, Work/Career, or Wealth/Success)
      for my highest good and greatest joy."

Sample questions about Love/Relationships

Here are some sample questions about love and relationships phrased in such a way as to obtain the clearest answer from The Enchanted Astrologer:

- Tell me what I need to know now about finding my soul mate for my highest good and greatest joy.

- Tell me what I need to know now about what is really going on in my relationship with _____.

- Tell me what I need to know now to improve my relationship with _____.

- Tell me what I need to know now about whether or not to end my relationship with _____.

- Tell me what I need to know now about my relationship with my child(ren).

- Tell me what I need to know now about my attitude towards love and relationships.

- Tell me what I need to know now about how to bring more love into my life.

Sample questions about Work/Career

Here are some sample questions about work and career phrased in such a way as to obtain the clearest answer from *The Enchanted Astrologer*:

- ✳ Tell me what I need to know now about what career path I should follow.

- ✳ Tell me what I need to know now about finding the best job for me.

- ✳ Tell me what I need to know now about getting a promotion.

- ✳ Tell me what I need to know now about getting a better paying job.

- ✳ Tell me what I need to know now about dealing with my boss.

- ✳ Tell me what I need to know now about dealing with that co-worker who is so difficult to work with.

- ✳ Tell me what I need to know now about how to deal with the problems at my company.

- ✳ Tell me what I need to know now about getting my career moving again.

- ✳ Tell me what I need to know now about changing careers.

Sample questions about Wealth/Success

Here are some sample questions about attaining wealth and success phrased in such a way as to obtain the clearest answer from *The Enchanted Astrologer*:

- ✳ Tell me what I need to know now about the best way for me to make more money.

- ✳ Tell me what I need to know now about whether or not I will make money if I _____.

❀ Tell me what I need to know now about getting the money to invest in _____.

❀ Tell me what I need to know now about whether I will be successful if I _____.

❀ Tell me what I need to know now about the best way for me to be more successful.

❀ Tell me what I need to know now about my attitude towards wealth and success.

❀ Tell me what I need to know now about improving my financial situation.

❀ Tell me what I need to know now about what is holding me back from being more wealthy and successful.

Visualize your question

Once you have decided what you want to ask about and how you would like to phrase your question, pick up the deck, and start shuffling it. As you shuffle, ask your question, either silently to yourself or out loud. As you say your question, see the situation you are asking about in your mind's eye. It might help you to close your eyes to do this. As you shuffle and ask your question, see your situation as if you are watching the action on a movie, TV, or computer screen. This technique is called "visualization," and it is very powerful.

If you are asking about meeting your soul mate or working with someone new or someone you have never met, see yourself and the form of that person but with a question mark hovering where their face should be.

If you are asking about someone you already know, then see yourself with that person and see their face, but see the question mark hovering above their head.

If you are asking about a new job situation, see in your mind's eye whatever you know about it or whatever you can guess about it from your life or work experience and, once again, see a question mark hovering over the part of the scene that you want to know about.

If you are asking about improving your financial situation or otherwise becoming more successful, visualize yourself doing the kind of thing that you will be doing when you make more money and gain more success. You can see yourself doing as many things as you would like to do. They can be as grand and extravagant as you can imagine. While you are seeing them, see a dollar sign and a question mark hovering above the situation.

How and why visualization works

When you visualize a situation, you are speaking to your subconscious mind in the language it understands; i.e., pictures and symbols, the language of our dreams. Your subconscious mind is the part of you that has to do with your tendencies to work either for or against your stated goals. If you have ever wondered why you do not do what you say you want to do, like lose weight, make more money, find the right partner, or improve your life in any way, the answer lies in your subconscious mind. If you are experiencing a conflict between your stated goals and your actions, it is usually because you have unconsciously sent your subconscious mind a clear indication that you have a reason to act against what your conscious mind says.

This kind of conflict is found to some degree or another in almost everyone who lives the frenetic pace and disconnected lifestyle of what Amy and I call "The Now Age." It seems that everything has to be done now. There is no longer the cushion of time between tasks and the gentle, loving support of family and friends to help us recover from the myriad daily assaults on our senses and our peace of mind. Our society has taken the ancient Zen Buddhist goal of "living in the moment" and stood it on its head, to the point where people live so much in the moment that they become disconnected from the world, both in general and from friends, family, co-workers, lovers, and even from themselves. Information overload and lack of personal time makes meaningful social interactions difficult and political action seem impossible.

Using The Enchanted Astrologer and the power of visualization creates a healing ritual space in your life. It enables you to reconnect with how you feel about what is happening to you. It also reminds you that your actions and inactions have gotten you to where you are now; you have the power to take new actions to get yourself to where you want to go. By using The Enchanted Astrologer to help make better decisions, you can help yourself to become yourself fully and to live the life you have always dreamed of.

This is not magic, though the results can often seem that way. When you are focused on your goal and not wasting precious resources working against your own best interests, your actions can produce the results you desire in the most efficient way possible.

When to stop shuffling the cards

There are many ways to decide when to stop shuffling and which is the card you are going to pick and they are all the right way to do it. There is no wrong way.

Most people keep shuffling until they have said their question once, twice, or any number of times that they are comfortable with. Some use a favorite or lucky number of times to ask the question before they choose their card, usually less then ten times. S o m e people add the figure of someone they love and trust, either living or passed on, to the scene of their question they see in their mind's eye. It could also be the image of an Angel, a religious figure, a great astrologer, a holy person, a powerful magician, a shaman of a

culture they resonate with, their spirit guide, or a figure that is allowed to materialize in its own form. They wait until that trusted, comforting figure makes a meaningful gesture indicating that the answer is now ready.

Whichever way you choose to decide when to stop shuffling, the most important thing is that you remember that there is no wrong way to do it. Trust in your own ability to do it correctly and you will not be disappointed. Do your best not to dwell on what answer you will get; that will stop the flow of the process of obtaining your answer.

How to choose your card

Once again, there are many ways to select the card that will answer your question and they are all the right way. There is no wrong way. As long as you have come to this point following the above instructions, you cannot go wrong.

The most important thing to remember in choosing your card is to keep seeing in your mind's eye the image of the situation you are asking about as you select your card. In fact, it is more important to see this image as you select your card than to see it as you are shuffling. I will explain why.

The new and fairly complex Chaos Theory in science explains the reason *The Enchanted Astrologer* gives you a useful answer. In a great example of prediction, Chaos Theory was very elegantly explained many years before its discovery by the pioneering psychologist, Karl Jung in his Theory of Synchronicity (from the Greek syn meaning "together" and chronos meaning "time"), or the Theory of Meaningful Coincidence. He formulated this theory to explain the uncanny "coincidences" that occur in our lives, but it also explains why divination systems like the tarot, astrology, and especially *The Enchanted Astrologer* give accurate answers. Jung said that things occurring at the same moment have a relationship of significance, if not of actual causality.

In other words, at the moment when you are asking your question with the strong intention of getting an answer, your answer is contained in the world around you, just as a piece of a hologram, those remarkable images that appear to be three dimensional, contains all of the information to recreate the whole hologram. As you asked your question, seeing your situation in your mind's eye to maximize your intention, you could see your answer by interpreting the shape of a cloud, the way the wind was blowing the trees and plants,the direction of a bird's flight, or any number of images that you would have to interpret. This is the way many indigenous peoples around the world get answers to their deep and burning questions — they love and trust the natural world so much that they know that when they ask their world for answers, they will get them.

The Enchanted Astrologer has been purposefully designed to answer your questions. It is a kind of sacred machine that makes it much easier for you to obtain the answers to your questions then to read the signs of nature around you as you ask your questions. It is designed for the fast pace and mainly indoor life of our modern age, though it can also be used outdoors. Amy's gorgeous fabric collage tapestry images on the cards of The Enchanted Astrologer deck are meant to mimic nature's ability to put us in a state of relaxed concentration and contemplation. The beauty of her art enchants our soul and revives our spirit, breathing new life into our hopes, dreams, and wishes for the future.

This is why it is so important that you see your situation in your mind's eye as you select your card. Seeing your situation as you choose the card enables the "meaningful coincidence" to occur.

Some people just cut the deck and take the card whose face is revealed as the card indicating their answer. The advantage of doing it this way is that it is very easy to do while you are shuffling. You do not have to put the cards down or even look at them until you have cut the deck and can see your card.

Some people like to take the top card, while others prefer to use the bottom card. Some people like to spread the shuffled deck out on a level surface and see which card "calls" to them. As long as your intention is strong and your mind is concentrated on the ritual of obtaining your answer, you will get the perfect answer to your question. The only things that could prevent this would be if you were very worried about the answer you were going to get or overly attached to a particular kind of answer, or thinking about something else when you were supposed to be concentrating on your question. If you are anxious, distracted, or intoxicated you will not get accurate information.

We all would prefer to hear only great news every day, but sometimes we have to wait and deal with what life has brought us. It is important to remember that we have all lived through quite a number of challenges that we worried so much about and doubted we could endure. Yet, somehow, we did endure. In most cases, nothing is ever as good as you think it is going to be and nothing is ever as bad as you think it is going to be. So take heart and ask your question in that state of relaxed contemplation, knowing that whatever answer you get you can deal with, and that *The Enchanted Astrologer* will offer helpful guidance to deal with any difficult situation.

How to obtain your answer

After you have finished feeding your soul by meditating awhile on the richly beautiful fabric collage tapestry that Amy made to symbolize the meaning of the Sign, Planet, or House card that you have selected, you are ready to obtain your answer. Turn to the index on pages 6-11 and look up the name of the card you selected. Below it, you will find the page number corresponding to the type of question you asked, either Love/Relationship, Work/Career, or Wealth/Success. Then turn to that page and there you will find your answer. It is really that simple to use.

To help you find your page as easily as possible, the Answer Pages section of *The Enchanted Astrologer* have been further broken down into three sections, the Signs of the zodiac, the Planets of astrology, and the Houses of a horoscope chart. You will know which section you are in and what page number you are looking at by looking at the vertical bar of purple color along the side of each of the Answer Pages section. The Signs section is indicated by the vertical bar of color running along the side of the top third of that section's pages, the Planets section by the bar running along the side of the middle third of the that section's pages, and the Houses section by the bar running along the side of the lower third of that section's pages.

These vertical bars of color from the Sign, Planet, and House sections bleed off the edge of the pages to create a visual aid for you. Even when *The Enchanted Astrologer* book is closed, it will be easy for you to know where the Sign, Planet, and House sections are. You probably will not be using this visual aid much at first because you will mainly be using the index. However, after awhile, you may use the color bars to quickly turn to the section containing the answers for the card you have chosen.

You will find a full page of text explaining the meaning of the card you have chosen for the type of question you have asked. Your answer is within that text. It could be the entire text that applies, but it is more likely that only a part of the text directly relates to your question. However, the part of the answer that related directly to your question will be an answer that may jump out at you. It may only be a word or a phrase, but you will see what *The Enchanted Astrologer* is trying to tell you. This may sound as if it is impossible, but when you ask your first question, you will see what I mean. If you are reading the page containing your answer with an open mind, you will hear it loud and clear. The words sometimes seem to speak to your innermost being, articulating feelings that resonate and affirm what you really know is true.

One of the great benefits of using an oracle like *The Enchanted Astrologer* is that it helps you to develop your intuition. We spend years of our lives trying to develop our minds in school, but few people spend any time at all developing their intuition. This is truly a pity because when our rational, logical mind is aided by our intuition, then and only then are we really experiencing life to the fullest. Our decisions become better and that helps us to avoid many problems and live better on practically every level.

It is important to remember that the answer you obtain is the answer to your question at the time you are asking. Simply reading your answer is going to have an effect on how you feel about the situation you are asking about and that is going to change your situation. Deciding to do something about your situation is going to change it even more. Actually taking action, whether that is to change your attitude, your behavior, your job, or anything else, will change your situation in countless ways. After you have taken steps to change your situation, do not be surprised if the next time you ask your question you get a different answer, revealing the next stage of your process or path to your goal. It is a little like peeling an onion; it takes a while to get to the core and sometimes you cry a little, but everything ends up tasting better in the end.

Developing your intuition

Intuition is like a muscle and can be made stronger from being properly exercised. The best way to exercise your intuition is to use it consciously. When you learn to use and, most importantly, to trust your intuition, it will keep getting stronger and stronger. We call a person with an extraordinarily developed mind a genius and we call a person with an extraordinarily developed intuition a psychic.

Both of these special groups of people are fairly rare in our society, but their very existence is a reminder of the power of our brains. Scientists seem to be fond of saying how small a percentage of our brain's real abilities and power we actually use. I would like to suggest that one of the reasons studies show this is because a large part of the brain that we are not using is connected with the abilities associated with our intuition. Unless we believe that we even have these abilities, how can we use them? That is why for most people, intuition comes in flashes — hunches, "gut" feelings, premonitions, or in precognitive dreams when the culturally supported "tyranny" of our rational mind is absent and our intuition is free to work for us.

However, even though most people have them, most people do not listen to their hunches, "gut" feelings, premonitions, and precognitive dreams. How many times have you heard someone say they wish they would have listened to that little voice inside that was telling them to do or not do something? How many times have you been the person saying that? Now that you are using *The Enchanted Astrologer*, you are taking an important and powerful step towards fully developing your intuition. As you keep "exercising" it, you will learn to trust it more.

Here is how to do it. As I said, some of the text is going to seem to jump out at you, a word, a phrase, a sentence, a paragraph, and sometimes the whole page will seem to be speaking directly in answer to your question. Just read your answer with an open mind and see if you start to "free associate" with what is said. This is probably one of the best ways to develop your intuition.

The way to free associate is as simple as it is powerful. When you read your answer, try to expand on what the words mean to you. For example, if you read the word "flight," let that word bring up as many images as come to you. The word flight can mean traveling on an airplane, but it can also mean to escape, as in "to take flight," it's what birds do, symbolizing freedom, and it is a word that can have personal meaning to you for any number of reasons. It could be a word from a favorite song, book, or even from the title of these things.

You get the picture, literally. When you read your answer from *The Enchanted Astrologer*, you will see pictures in your mind's eye, just as surely as you did when you asked your question. Only, when you asked your question, you put the images there and when you get your answer, the images come to you in their own way, shape, and form. This is how intuition works. True, some intuitive people actually see or hear words or even complete sentences. However, most people, even some of the most successful psychics, "only" see pictures or symbols with special meanings to them. The reason they are successful is because they know how to interpret those symbols. The reason they know how to do this is because, through practice, they have learned what these symbols mean and how to trust their ability to interpret them.

If your answer is unclear to you

There are going to be times when the answer you receive does not seem to be related to the question you have asked. These are actually the best times to make fast progress in the development of your intuition. When your answer seems unclear, try to mentally rise above your situation and, instead of seeing it in your mind's eye, as it was when you asked your question, see it from outside the location where you saw it taking place, possibly from above it or from another country. See it as if you were an alien from another country or even another planet, or a very young child asking for the situation to be explained to you. Then go back and read your answer again. You may find that what you read before now has new meanings for you, or that you are now able to free-associate the words with other things that do explain your answer. Thinking "outside of the box" can give you new perspectives on your situation.

If your answer is still unclear, you may want to re-read the meaning of the Planet, Sign, or House that you have selected. Or read its other meanings. For example, if you asked about Wealth/Success but your answer seems unclear, read the Love/Relationship and Work/Career answers, too. If doing all these things does not help you to know your answer, you might want to ask a person that you love and trust to help you interpret it.

Using The Enchanted Astrologer with others

When you use The Enchanted Astrologer with other people, you are going to have a lot of fun, especially if you insist that everyone asks their questions out loud. Of course, if people have questions that they do not want to share, you must honor their wishes. However, everyone has at least one question that they can ask out loud. Sharing in this way can help us to learn so much about our similarities as well as our differences, and help us to empathize and be more understanding of each other.

Everyone who uses The Enchanted Astrologer should treat it as an experiment. Give it a chance. Read these directions to everyone, follow them, then see what happens. If one or more of your group is openly skeptical, do not let that stop your session. There is an old saying, "The Truth is not afraid of questions." We are confident enough in The Enchanted Astrologer to use it with practically anyone, anytime, anywhere.

Remind anyone who says he is a skeptic that the dictionary defines a skeptic as a person who is not sure of something and is investigating to see what is true or false, not as someone who knows beyond a doubt that something like astrology and divination cannot be true. As the great British naturalist, Sir Thomas Huxley said, "I'm too much of a skeptic not to believe that anything is possible."

If your skeptical guest(s) approach using The Enchanted Astrologer as a scientific experiment, it will help them to be in the right frame of mind to receive their answer. Many times, it is the skeptics who end up asking question after question.

Once you have read the instructions and started using *The Enchanted Astrologer*, you will all be talking about the things that really matter to you, not engaging in the usual superficial conversations that you find at most social gatherings. That is, for most people, an unusual and incredibly powerful experience to begin with. You will probably find that people will reveal things to the group that they would ordinarily never tell anyone. Remember to be respectful of the information that is revealed. Think of yourself as a counselor, someone who has a sacred duty towards those she or he advises. If you want your own secrets kept, keep those of other people.

It is almost guaranteed that if you use *The Enchanted Astrologer* in a group, everyone is going to give and get a lot of advice. Sometimes, especially when someone does not immediately understand the meaning of the answer they have received, other people will try to impose on the person who asked the question what they think the answer means.

If you are that person and you know that the other people using *The Enchanted Astrologer* with you have your best interests at heart, then listen to what they have to say with an open mind. They may be correct. However, and I cannot state this strongly enough, you must remember that this is your question and your answer. The answer that you received is not simply the words in the book, it is your reaction to those words, your free-associations, and your intuitive leaps that enable you to learn and grow. I am not saying that you should be closed minded, but I am saying that you should be working on becoming as humbly self-confident and honest with yourself as you can be. If you are, then you can have faith in your answer and thank everyone else for his or her concern. Do not get angry if they insist that they know your answer better than you do. To get angry would be a sign that your self-confidence was lacking and that they were actually correct.

We have created *The Enchanted Astrologer* to help you find the answers to your questions, to help you develop your intuition, and thereby to improve your decision-making ability, all while you are having fun. What could be better? It is in no way meant to be a substitute for your own decision-making ability or for the advice of a licensed professional counselor and advisor.

Remember, the common denominator of all human-caused suffering is poor decision-making. It is our sincere desire that *The Enchanted Astrologer* will help you to make better decisions so that you, too, may live a life of quality and meaning.

SIGNS

♈ ARIES

Aries is considered the first sign of the zodiac. Arians, as children of Aries are called, can seem aggressive and forceful because they are trying to be independent. They like to be pioneers in some way, the first to do something. They want to do things in an original way. Even the way they are original can sometimes defy categorization. If anyone can spontaneously create a new way to be a pioneer, it is an Aries. They certainly don't like to be second or even to wait for anything for very long. They function best when they act on their first impulse and don't second-guess themselves. They hate lies and liars and can sometimes be too honest for their own good.

The symbol for Aries is the headstrong Ram. Each spring the desire to mate and stake his claim to his territory drives the Ram to display his bravery by butting heads with his competitors. After a few times, the one who can handle the headache and hasn't given up is the winner. People born under the sign of Aries share a lot in common with their symbol, the Ram. They are willing to butt heads with those they think are standing in their way. Sometimes they will give up if they do not get their own way quickly enough.

The reason why Arians are sometimes not as brave, original, and pioneering as they wish they were is because people do not arrive in the world already an expert in the things their sun sign is known for. They have come into this world with the challenge of the astrological sign Aries because they want to learn how to accomplish something that has never been done before and accomplish it without letting fear stand in their way.

The lesson for Arians is that they must learn the hardest part of how to be brave. No Arian wants to think that she is letting fear stop her. However, since Arians are learning what it takes to be uncompromising individuals, they are, in effect, learning all the various aspects of what it means to be brave. Arians are more afraid of being afraid than they are afraid of any actual person, situation or thing. This is the central challenge for all born under the sign Aries and it is also why they sometimes suffer from panic attacks. They must keep in mind that any fears or self-doubts that are triggered in them are not signs of weakness, loosing control, or a guarantee of failure. They must not let fear of feeling any signs of fear in themselves paralyze them into inaction and even more self-doubt.

At their most basic level, our fears are a means of preventing us from getting hurt physically, emotionally, and financially. Fear is meant to keep us from repeating mistakes and to keep us out of harm's way. It is as natural an emotion as love; in fact, they are opposites. Negative fears are those that are irrational and counterproductive. They exist to challenge us into developing methods for coping with them. When we do, the memory of our negative fears enables us to see how strong we have become. An Aries could not prove his strength to himself unless he first became aware of his fears and then learned to deal with them. I purposefully do not say, "overcome" or "eliminate" when it comes to fear. As a natural emotion, fear will always be with us. Fear is not a sign of weakness, but giving in to your fears is.

LOVE/RELATIONSHIPS — *Aries*

If you do not have a partner now, one may be coming into the picture very soon. The delay may be a result of issues surrounding honesty. Either you or your past partners were too honest or not honest enough. Or the relationships of those you care about could have been hurt or destroyed by dishonesty.

Do not let your fears protect you to the point that you live your life alone, unless that is really what you want to do. All your fears and those of your partners must be faced, understood, and dealt with now or they will work to undermine your relationships. Give voice to all the original ideas and feelings you both have been keeping inside for so long. Even if you end up butting heads a bit, it is time to get everything out in the open. Things are going to start happening a lot faster than you thought they would and anything other than honesty and directness is just not going to work.

It is time for you to bring the theme of "pioneering" to your relationships. Be the first to make your move and do not be afraid. If you are in a committed relationship, it is time to break new ground and take it to the next level. If you are looking for a relationship, you must go looking for it and in places where you have never been before. It may even be a great time to go on a trip that you might normally consider too lacking in creature comforts for you to enjoy. It is time to test and prove yourself and your relationship in a new way.

Any complexity in your relationships will not fare well now. It is time to simplify your love life and all of your relationships.

WORK/CAREER — *Aries*

At this time, issues of honesty can either make or break your work situation and possibly even your career. Try and be as honest as you can without exposing yourself to unnecessary trouble. Being too honest or headstrong can be as dangerous as being dishonest now. Strive for balance. No matter how it seems, you are on your own now and thinking that you have to defend other people may backfire.

The challenge may be that other people are being dishonest or too honest and you might be drawn up into the mess they are making. If so, make sure that any dishonesty is dealt with appropriately. However, be careful to extricate yourself from the situation as quickly but as carefully as you can. You have to show everyone that you are honest and your own person, not part of any group. It is time to act like a pioneer and go off on your own — a living pioneer, not one with arrows sticking out of his back.

It does get a bit lonely when you are committed to doing things in your own unique way. Those who are insecure about their own abilities may see your display of willpower as a threat. However, when others see that you know what you are doing, they will understand your actions for what they are, the actions of an uncompromising individualist. It is time to stick up for your own interests and put yourself first. Any arguments you find yourself in are a sign that you are wasting your time and energy explaining yourself when you could be blazing new and exciting career trails.

You need the freedom to be able to act on your instincts. You need to be able to take full credit for the successes and failures that are a natural part of any business or career.

WEALTH/SUCCESS — *Aries*

The image to see in your mind's eye is that you are a pioneer starting out on an adventure to seek your fortune. You may not know exactly how or where or when, but you know you are on your way. This is a good time to start your own business. Take action immediately to investigate businesses you can start yourself, without necessarily giving up the support of the job you have now. Do not rush and you will get that business up and running sooner than you think.

Do not tell everybody what you are trying to achieve; they would not really understand your real goals and motives. Many would watch you closely to see if your every move was in keeping with your stated goals. They would view challenges as obstacles and not as the stepping-stones to wealth and success that all lessons are. That would get in your way and slow you down. Share your ideas only with those who have proven they are as honest as you and worthy of your trust.

This is a lucrative time when you are favored to receive awards and win contests where your individual skills are involved. Matters of chance are not as strongly favored as matters where you have to do something which no one else can do better or faster. It is a time where you will be recognized for your accomplishments as an individual. Do not enter any contests with anyone else. It is not a time for you to be a part of a wealth-building team. This is a time for you and your abilities to shine and pay off handsomely.

Be mindful that you may have an unconcious fear of success. If you are aware of this, you will be less likely to sabotage opportunities for success. Remember your true gifts, your loved ones, and appreciate that for the wealth that it is.

♉

TAURUS

People born under the sign of Taurus share a lot in common with their symbol, the Bull. Although they are usually patient and gentle, when pushed too far, a Taurian can become like a bull tormented by a toreador's cape. Angry or not, they are so set on their goal that they can see little or nothing else. In fact, they sometimes think they must be equally set on the way they will accomplish their mission.

Taurians seem to be able to cope with just about anything that gets in their way. In fact, many people born under the sign of Taurus are sources of mystery and awe to their friends because no one except a Taurus will exert the energy necessary to put up with a situation most other signs would just walk away from. But Taurians don't even like to walk around a situation let alone walk away from one. Meeting challenging situations requiring patience and endurance is how they prove their abilities to themselves and those around them.

Taurians get the material comforts they need and overcome obstacles by exerting their immense power in a sustained and methodical manner, no matter who or what tries to make them give up on their efforts or even deviate from their plan. They function best when they are able to concentrate and stick to a preconceived plan, especially when they know their reward will be pleasure and luxury.

The reason why Taurians are sometimes not as determined, patient, and comfortably well off as they wish they were is because people do not arrive in the world already experts in the things their sun sign is known for. They have come into this world with the challenge of the astrological sign Taurus because they want to learn how to be determined, patient, comfortably well off or wealthy, and how to cope with everything those things require.

If Taurians really want to possess what they desire, they must learn to include in their plan to achieve their goal at least some room for flexibility and change because sometimes the best way to get what they want is to modify and adjust their plan of attack to the circumstances in which they find themselves. It is not enough to be a stubborn bull if you want to be a successful one.

Taurians will often stubbornly cling to a plan, a belief, or a person even when all the evidence points to the fact that it would be best to change that plan and belief or not see that person anymore. The reason is their fear of giving up, being proved wrong, and wasting their time. There is also the fear of having to face the unpredictable unknown and go through the struggle of coming up with a new plan, finding a new person, and having to learn a whole new way to proceed that is often strong enough to cause Taurians to stay when they should go, and to fight when they should switch.

Taurians are, by nature, very resistant to listening to any advice that they think is not in agreement with the plan they have already decided on. That could include the advice contained here in *The Enchanted Astrologer*. What good is advice if a person has already decided that what he or she believes to be the way is the only way? There is a saying; "There are none so blind as those who will not see." You do not have to make big changes, but you do have to be open to change, such as to the suggestions in this book. Remember, change is the evidence of the existence of life.

LOVE/RELATIONSHIPS — *Taurus*

If you do not have a relationship now, it may be because you are too stubborn or are so afraid of stubborn people that you deny yourself the pleasure of anyone who appears stubborn to you, even though he or she may just be very self-confident or knowledgeable.

Take things slowly now. Be practical. Make a plan. At this time, you have to be patient with your partners, at least those who deserve your patience, and they have to be patient with you. If this is a stressful time and you both are trying your best to deal with it, then you can allow for thoughtless behavior. However, if one of you is using his or her situation as a crutch or a weapon, then the relationship is going to be unpleasant. There may come a breaking point where an ugly argument ensues. This will be a test of your patience and kind nature.

You most likely will not break up because Taurus is the sign of the person who copes with difficult situations almost as a trial by fire. However, if you keep the relationship going longer then you should and then you decide to end it, the emotional toll on you both will be far greater than if you broke up when you really should have. If you are financially well off, you are not likely to split from your partner if it involves splitting your resources and diminishing your lifestyle and if you lack money, it will be difficult to leave. If either of you now is expecting to be supported financially, realize that expectation can cause resentment and can work against the supported person's spirit of independence and self-esteem.

It is very important that anyone you partner with shares your tastes and desires in life. If you like deluxe comfort and your partner likes to camp out, there will eventually be a parting of the ways.

WORK/CAREER — *Taurus*

At this time your career is flowing along better than you think. Unseen forces, those that you set in motion and some that you have no idea about, are causing movement in your career, though it may not be apparent to you or to those around you. It is a time to be patient and practical. See the developments in your career now as being like the first flowers of spring — though things may appear gray and cold, there is movement beneath the surface. You may not realize how beautiful things are going to be until things start popping up like those first flowers, appearing as if by magic.

Rewards are possible for you now, but in the form of you being valued for your abilities, steady hand, and consistent contributions. This is a time of preparation for the promotions and bonuses to come, rather than for the actual promotions and bonuses. Do not stray from the course you know to be the right one for you.

Help to strengthen and consolidate things at work, rather than trying to do things differently. Slow and steady is the way to proceed now. It is the best way to increase your power and prestige. Now is the time to stick to a well-described routine or the plan of a superior. It is not the right time to jump into any great master plan for action. For the near future, work where you are allowed to devote a reasonable amount of time to ensuring that the value of people, places and things is being correctly assessed.

If you are between jobs, one is coming soon. Occupations with which you could do well now include transportation, construction, conservation, landscaping, farming, engineering, design, mathematics, and the fine arts—especially sculpture, fashion, music, and singing.

WEALTH/SUCCESS — *Taurus*

This is a time for you to attain any reward you have been working for diligently and patiently. Even if it seems that you are not able to get all you had hoped for, it is time to be pragmatic and to take what you can get now. If you have not deviated from the plan you made, you can expect to reap the rest of what you have sown later.

Now is the time to go slow but steadily. Conserve your resources for another day. Put money in safe and secure investments now, including savings accounts, and you will do better than by taking chances. This is not the best time for risk taking or gambling. You may win a contest where the prize is awarded for perseverance or beauty, or in a contest where you had to keep renewing your entry again and again. You may also be recognized for sticking with something others had given up on. If you are physically able to participate in tests of endurance, you would do better now than at other times. Also favored are matters involving art, beauty, long-term investments, farming, gardening, and all other pursuits where your ability to make things look good is crucial.

This is a time for patience with younger people, and the slow and steady approach will work best. In fact, they may be the ones who bring home the prizes mentioned above. In your dealings with children, stress safety and sticking with established goals.

Spend some time every day appreciating the beauty in life and the beauty in your life. Be grateful for your senses if you are fortunate enough to be able to see, feel, taste, hear, or smell.

GEMINI

Those born under the sign Gemini are among the best com-
municators of information, especially their opinions and things
that they have heard. They do not gossip any more than most people; they are just better at it and enjoy it more. You can bet that
when a Gemini tells you something, it is the most up-to-date information available.

Yet, though they speak clearly and put their point across, they
are often misunderstood. Most people want to be known for their
unwavering commitment to a bunch of opinions about what is true
about life. In fact, most people think that is what everyone has to
be to function in the world, but Geminis do not think that way. They

are curious to know what life is and they are more than willing to adjust their beliefs when information that appeals to them comes along.

They want to experience life and in as many different ways as they can. They may even go so far as to have something of a double life. At the very least, they have two opinions about everything, more if they have actually studied a particular subject in depth. They will do practically anything to avoid being bored, which, to a Gemini, is almost a fate worse than death.

Because they are interested in everything, Geminis become skilled at anything they put their lightning quick minds to. They are also the most versatile of signs. It is a rare Gemini that only does one thing extremely well. They also have great dexterity.

Geminis do not just have two or three opinions; it is more like they are two or three different people and that has to be accepted by those who want to be close to them. Their changeability can be annoying or interesting, depending on how much you want people to be the same every time you see them.

Geminis love to be up on the latest things and they try their best to know something about everything. This is the origin of stories about their legendary curiosity. Geminis think that if they only had the time and access to enough information, they could actually come to know everything. Nobody can give the appearance of knowing everything better than a Gemini, though sometimes they may find themselves arguing the exact opposite position of the one they held yesterday. This is a source of their charm. They also provide the rest of us a valuable service by reminding us not to be so certain that our truth is the only truth.

People who are just getting to know a Gemini may try to pin him down and consequently may think that Gemini changed his mind too often. This is just how it appears on the surface. Geminis do not actually change their minds so much as they actually have two minds, just as our brains are divided into two hemispheres. Many thousand years ago, the ancient sages were wise to pick as the symbol for Gemini a pair of twins. For it is as if within them there are actually two different people with two different sets of values and opinions — maybe more. In fact, Geminis are legendary for functioning best when they have two or more things to do at the same time.

However, the lesson for Geminis to learn is that there is an important reason why they are not as knowledgeable, quick, versatile, and skillful as they wish they were. They have come into this world with the astrological sign Gemini because they want to learn everything, especially how to be quick, versatile, skillful, and smart!

LOVE/RELATIONSHIPS — *Gemini*

If you do not have a love relationship now, it is important that, even when you are flirting, you present yourself to others in a fairly consistent manner. Make sure that your love interest is not two-faced or superficial. Avoid seeming impatient or desperate.

You may find that you are interested in more than one person now, even if you are in a committed relationship. It is also possible that more than one person is interested in you. There may be quite a difference in your age, station in life, or educational background and that of your new partner(s).

You have to spend a lot of time now relating to many people at the same time, either in person or via telephone, fax, computer, or otherwise. Jealousy may arise because you are flirting or not home or paying a lot of attention to others around you.

Problems may also arise because you, your partner, or both of you have been acting like two different people. This makes trust difficult if not impossible and gives rise to fear and suspicion. It is important that you both feel like you know and trust each other.

If you both trust and respect each other and there are still difficulties between you, the problem may be that you are not communicating well. Both of you must listen as if the other might be saying something important. Avoid the tendency to think about what you are going to say next when your partner is talking. Keep talking to each other even if you get into an argument.

This is a time when reading, writing, learning, and growing must be an important part of any relationship you are involved in. Taking courses or developing your skills together can improve your relationship.

WORK/CAREER — *Gemini*

If your work or career is boring or not challenging enough for your skill level, the best way to deal with it is to stay at your job while planning and taking action to change jobs or even to change careers. The time you could spend daydreaming about your new line of work might actually help you find a way to improve your experience of your present job in several ways and you might even find changing jobs unnecessary. For this to happen, you would have to be able use everything you know in a display of your versatility.

If your work is satisfying to you, then you may want to start branching out or doing a second job. At this time, doing two jobs could be easier and more beneficial than doing only one. You may want to go to school or take on-the-job training.

No matter what you do, now is the time to learn or craft new techniques to streamline your work and make sure that the path to your career goals is clear. Study as much as you can about your job and where you want to be in three years. Become part of any information exchanges in your industry so that you can stay abreast of the latest information and methods for doing your job. However, it would greatly benefit you to study what is going on in your whole industry and related industries.

It is time to become aware of your prejudices and preconceived notions and do your best to rid yourself of them. It is important to look beneath the surface of people and their actions to understand why they are acting the way they are. You will usually find that it is nothing personal against you; they are only trying to better their own situations.

Wealth/Success — *Gemini*

It is possible to be wealthy and not feel wealthy. This is your present situation. In many ways, you are better off than ever, yet arriving at this point in your life has taken its toll and opened your eyes to aspects of life that you only imagined before. Instead of celebrating what you have done and how far you have come, you are anxious about attaining even more wealth and success. This can make you feel quite moody, dejected, and depressed one minute and happy the next when you remember where you used to be.

It is a waste of time to envy anyone else or imagine that her situation is better than our own. We all have our challenges. Yours is now to accept how much better off you are than many other people and to motivate yourself to improve without belittling yourself for the things you have not yet accomplished.

It is important that you speak like someone who is wealthy and successful a bit more than you actually are now. One of the reasons people do not allow wealth and success to come into their life is because they are not willing to go through the many changes that wealth and success bring. Acting "as if" will prepare you for the future. Too many people think that wealth and success will solve all their problems and refuse to realize that wealth and success bring in a whole host of problems most people cannot conceive of. This is why they do not attain them.

New wealth and success will probably come from two or more sources, or from an investment or opportunity associated with versatility, communications, infotainment, schooling, or from a brother, sister, or relative who is not your parent. Appreciate the wealth of having loving, supportive relatives in your life, if you are fortunate enough to have any.

CANCER

Those born under the astrological sign Cancer are well known for their ability to nurture others. They are especially sensitive to the ways people communicate their feelings and can be easily affected when there are bad feelings affecting those they care about. In fact, learning about feelings and the moods they produce are an important part of being a Cancer. In astrology, the Moon is considered a planet and associated with the sign Cancer. The Moon's ever-changing shape and its effect on the constantly shifting ocean tides is like our ever-changing moods, though the Moon's shape is a lot more predictable.

The past is very important to Cancerians. Their family history is especially so, either as a source of pride or as a painful experience affecting them as if it had just happened. Either way, they will always want to relate what is going on in the present moment to something they have known in the past. By sticking with what is familiar or relating the new to what they already feel familiar with, they are able to feel secure.

The symbol for Cancer is the crab. Feeling insecure makes them want to withdraw into their own version of a crab's protective shell.

The reason why Cancerians are sometimes not as secure, sensitive, and nurturing as they wish they were is because people do not arrive in the world already experts in the things their sun sign is known for. They have come into this world with the challenge of the astrological sign Cancer because they want to learn how to be secure, sensitive, and nurturing

Cancerians are legendary for their ability to nurture people and projects along, for they sense the needs of others on an emotional level. However, it is important that they remember that meeting their own emotional needs is just as important. Often, they have to be able to nurture themselves, for they are so good at nurturing others that others forget how Cancerians, too, need nurturing.

When feeling emotionally secure, there is no one who is more giving than a Cancer. However, when Cancerians feel emotionally insecure, they are totally unable to give and this can confuse those who have come to depend on them. Being shy, especially at those vulnerable times, a Cancerian would be reluctant to tell anyone of his needs for fear that those who he cares for would let him down. A Cancerian would be able to forgive a person who was unable to be there for her at a critical time, but she would never forget what had happened.

Cancerians are often affected by the time of day they decide to do something. Plans made at night become harder to make real in the daytime and vice versa. If they find themselves forgetting to put the plans of last night into practice the next day, they must be as patient and forgiving of themselves as they would be with the mistakes made by a child learning and growing.

Before anyone can help others, she or he has to feel secure. The first rule of warfare is "make your base secure." Without a good foundation no home will last very long.

Cancerians would do well to remember that they may not be as strong as those around them think they are, but they are certainly strong enough to do what has to be done to make their dreams come true. They must resist withdrawing into their shell if they start to feel insecure. Their usual courage, patience, and gentle energy are more than they will need to make their life what they will.

LOVE/RELATIONSHIPS — *Cancer*

If you do not have a relationship now, the problem is related to the issues of mothering and nurturing. You may be looking for someone to take care of you or you may be repelled by anyone who needs to be taken care of in some way. Or it may be hard to find a partner who shares your views on children and child rearing.

What you need now is to know that you are with someone who loves you and whom you can depend on. You need to be supported and nurtured and loved unconditionally. You, in turn, need to nurture your partner and to make him or her feel safe. If you are not with someone right now, be on the lookout for a person who embodies these loving, gentle qualities. If that kind of relationship is not attractive to you, be aware that your own upbringing may have been dysfunctional and you are now equating intensity, uncertainty, and even danger with passion and true love. You may be setting yourself up to avoid having a relationship that will last when desire and passion mature into commitment.

Not all people are capable of displaying their feelings as much as you would like them to. It would be a pity if your shyness or that of a potentially great partner for you prevented you from meeting someone whom you would come to love passionately and cherish. Sometimes a slow fire burns the longest.

If you live alone, but are in a relationship with someone whom you love and trust and who has proven himself worthy of your love and trust, it may be time to get serious about living together. However, if you find that your partner or someone you are interested in does not want to do the work necessary to make your relationship grow stronger, you should be thankful that you are finding out now while you still have time to do something about it.

WORK/CAREER — *Cancer*

It is quite possible that soon you will be doing more than just a job; you will feel more like you have found a home. Stick with what is familiar to you or to work that reminds you of the work done by you or your family in the past. Family and those who care deeply about you can help your job and career in some way. You may also work out of your home now.

The past is also important to the progression of your career at this time. Any work-related or career mistakes you have made in the past must be remembered and examined. It is not necessary for you to seek out all involved and make amends, though if they are still in your life, that would be a good thing to do. It is most important that you come to terms with your past so that you can feel secure enough to move forward the way you know you should.

The main theme for you now is actually the first rule of warfare: Make your base secure. Your self-protective instincts are very good now and you may even prefer a job in police work, security, or defense. The establishment of security requires a shrewd approach to everything you do. This shrewdness could help you do well in the world of finance, investment, or fundraising for both non-profit and profitable ventures.

Occupations that are favored at this time include those that enable you to address the needs of families, such as food, clothing, household items, real estate, and medicine. All things connected with younger people and children would be beneficial. You would do well with careers involving the nurturing of people and animals, and business projects struggling to survive their first few years of growing pains. .

Wealth/Success — *Cancer*

Wealth and success may manifest themselves in your life through the efforts of a close family member. You may gain in physical possessions and in other forms of wealth, too. You may find yourself placed in an important and powerful position by those you consider your family. If you are lucky enough to feel that your co-workers or even your boss is like family to you, then watch that area of your life for increased good fortune.

This is not a time to risk getting involved with anything that might make you feel insecure. Gambling is not favored now. There is benefit to be derived from staying where you are, rather than from moving on to something new. You should not distract yourself with the stress of moving now. It will prevent you from seeing the opportunities around you.

Past good deeds and people from your past may reward you now. People who you took care of or who took care of you may again become important in your life.

If there are any children in your life, this is the time to nurture and protect them financially. It is a time when being a little over-protective is called for. It is very important that you and your loved ones feel safe and protected because the important events that are about to unfold for your benefit need that security for them to be able to manifest themselves. As a side benefit, you may be surprised to learn new and very interesting information about family members both here and those who have passed over. You will be amazed how the issues of your grandparents will seem to have been miraculously transferred to the children in your life; although these issues will be modified for the times you now live in.

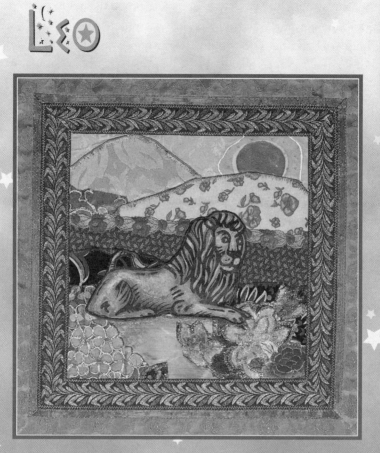

LEO

Leo is the sign of the creative organizers of the zodiac. Practically no one is as good as they are at recognizing the solution to a problem and organizing the means to solve it. It is this ability that gives rise to Leo's reputation as a great leader. Like all leaders, Leos feel more comfortable when they are telling others what has to be done rather than taking care of the routine details themselves. They get annoyed with themselves for this trait, but not for long, because Leos like themselves a lot. They put themselves where there is much that needs to be done, and they associate themselves with the right group of people so that their creative input is always welcome, even if they do not always jump in and get their hands dirty.

The symbol for Leo is the strong and proud male lion, a most appropriate symbol. Not only is a group of lions referred to as a "pride" of lions, but also the importance of personal pride to those born during the time of Leo cannot be overstated. They would not want to be connected to anyone or anything that they did not feel was up to their high personal standards. This inclines Leos to provide those born under the other signs of the zodiac with a good example.

Showing us all how things are done is a special gift possessed by Leos. This is why they have such a knack for drama. It can be acting, the arts and music, or any form of display. Their generosity requires them to create situations and objects that will benefit and entertain them and those they consider worthy to be connected with them.

The lesson for Leos to learn is that there is an important reason why they are not as proud, powerful, and as good leaders as they wish they were. They have come into the world when the Sun was in the astrological sign Leo because they want to learn the best way possible to become the kind of powerful leaders they can be proud to be. Sometimes, even the best of leaders must put on an act to get the job done.

Of course, when Leos are creating things for others to look at, their audience's feedback becomes very important to them. If their dramatic gestures are not acknowledged sufficiently, their pride will be hurt. Then they might forget their responsibilities to others and maybe even try to use their power to influence others in a dictatorial fashion.

Leos are legendary for their ability to help and protect those who acknowledge them as special people. They gain a sense of their own self-worth by giving what they think others need from them. However, it is important that they remember that they, too, need help and protection. Leos would usually be too prideful to ask for help.

Leos' reputation for having large egos comes from this inability to ask for help. When they put such obvious value on being helpful to others, yet don't ask for help, it is easy for others to think that Leos think they are either too good to ask for help, or that they don't think anyone has the ability to help someone as great, strong, and talented as a Leo.

Many Leos do mistakenly believe that anyone who needs help is weak and incapable of being a leader on his or her own; however, we all need help. Like the lion and other kings, Leos should get used to letting those who care about their welfare help them and bring them gifts for a change. No one knows how to live as royally as Leos do. When they learn how to accept help and to delegate their authority, then they can show the world how to really live the good life.

LOVE/RELATIONSHIPS — Leo

If you do not have a relationship, you soon will. It may or may not be the longest lasting, but it will definitely be one of the most memorable. You will know your new partner because everyone's head will turn when she or he enters a room. Your time together will be both romantic and dramatic. He or she will treat you like royalty and everyone else will treat you both like celebrities.

If you are in a good relationship, you can expect it to get even better. It will be one of the most romantic times of your lives. You will enjoy all kinds of fun things and creative expressions together, both your own and that of other people. You may find yourselves actively pursuing creative projects that you have been putting off for a long time. You could do it alone or both work on the same project. In either case, you would enjoy the mutual support. You could also attend creative classes together, visit museums, go to art galleries, movies, dance recitals, concerts, and the theater. A long vacation would be a perfect way to start this period of your life.

Any trouble in your relationships would be caused by problems related to organization, responsibility, and leadership. If one or both of you was unwilling to act responsibly or if one or both of you wanted to take a leadership role in your relationship, the result would be the same. A successful relationship is not one in which everything is split down the middle. It is one where each person does what he or she does best in a spirit of service to the other person. If you find that there are many essential tasks that neither of you is good at, then you must both try your best to do them together and not just try to boss each other around.

WORK/CAREER — Leo

It is time to get creative, no matter what your job or career. This requires you to look, in a new way, at what you are involved in. Do not just accept that you and those around you know the best way to accomplish a goal. Look at your situation as if you have never seen it before. Or bring in someone, maybe even a young person, and explain your problem to him or her. You may be surprised at the fresh look their eyes may provide for you.

You can have tremendous success with work requiring you to come up with creative ideas. Though mental work is usually associated with creativity, you can be quite creative in work requiring your physical labor. Your creativity can be expressed by coming up with the best way to do your job. Whatever you do, you should produce work that is a reflection of your unique personality and purpose in the world.

Producing this work is like giving birth to a child. Like childbirth, creativity does require the cooperation of those around you. If you actually find that there are those around you who are resisting your efforts to find creative ways to deal with career related situations, you must first use your new burst of creativity to find a way to convince them to let you try your hand at making things work.

A job in the traditionally creative fields like art, music, dance, acting, film, TV, writing, design, or fashion would be wonderful. There are opportunities around you to be creative in any job.

If you are between jobs now, do not waste time thinking that you have failed in some way. Use this time to look at your strengths and weaknesses and choose a job that allows you to do what you are best at. Do not settle for a job that merely allows you to do what you are good at or you will be plagued with the nagging feeling that you are not getting all you can out of life.

WEALTH/SUCCESS — Leo

At this time, you can expect to live more like royalty then ever before. If you have been working on a project that could pay you royalties, you can expect it to succeed. You may have finally gained enough wealth and success to stop worrying.

You stand to benefit tremendously by becoming involved with helping younger people or the child within you to grow and come to understand what life is all about. The best way to accomplish that would be through play. Teach them to think of achieving success as a game and to just have fun with it. If it is taken too seriously, success becomes a target that always gets farther and farther away.

Role-playing is another form of acting. If you have been having problems with your resources, try acting out the part of you that wants to be wealthy and successful and then playing the part of you that does not want to be successful. Both of those parts are in everyone.

You can benefit greatly now from performing, producing, or even watching performances, both live and via any and all forms of media. A brilliant idea could come to you as you are playing or watching. In this information age, ideas are the currency that will make many people rich. Your creative explorations can lead you to many marketable ideas.

Games — including sports, performing, creativity, and children — could benefit you now. They all contain an element of risk; they have a life of their own once they come into being. You are also in very good position to profit, not only from all these things, but also from taking a chance on a calculated risk or gamble. Investing, a more socially respectable form of gambling, is also favored at this time.

♍ VIRGO ✦

Virgo is the astrological sign associated with the myriad details of life. Virgos like to get things done. It is as if they are driven to perform useful acts to the best of their ability at all times, no matter how big or small the task. Virgos are very careful and methodical in everything they do because they value order and neatness. When involved with people or situations that are messy or disorganized, they will probably find themselves irritable and unable to apply themselves to the task at hand in their customarily efficient manner.

The symbol for Virgo is a young, virginal woman. This symbolizes the value placed by Virgos on purity of mind and body. In a way, they are always young, trying to learn all they can, and learning the way a young person would.

Developing their skill and confidence in themselves as hard-working people is more important to them than the praise of the crowd. However, they are not machines, and Virgos do need some thoughtful words of encouragement from those with whom they work and work for. A pat on the back and appreciation for a job well done will usually satisfy them more than fame or money.

The lesson for Virgos to learn is that there is an important reason why they are not as useful, skillful, and perfect as they wish they were. They have come into this world with the astrological sign Virgo because they want to learn the best way possible to be useful, skillful, and the best that they can be. Not perfect, but the best that they can be.

Many Virgos do not realize they are perfectionists of the highest order. Why? Because they feel that if they really were perfectionists, they would be much closer to perfection than they are! It goes to show what perfectionists Virgos can be.

The lesson for Virgos also involves the sign's legendary tendency to over-analyze and worry about things. Worry is actually a combination of two fears resulting from the very process of analysis. To analyze anything, you have to know as much as you can about it. However, to analyze a living person or an ongoing situation you are never going to have all the information you would like to have. The first fear that produces worry is that you do not have enough information to fully understand a situation. The second fear is that you will not be able to deal with the consequences of a situation unless you fully understand it and can predict what is going to happen.

When Virgos use *The Enchanted Astrologer*, they must avoid letting their tendency to worry about how things are going to turn out influence them too strongly. They have to suspend their tendency to criticize what they are going to be reading and hold it up to some impossible standard of perfection.

If they really want to be as practical as most Virgos would like to be, then they must realize that they will use their gift for criticism in a constructive way by waiting to use it until they have first listened to and absorbed the information they receive. They must stay out of their own way and not let their tendency to focus on some minor imperfection prevent them from hearing another part of their message that proves to be the key to help them unlock the door to life's glorious bounty.

LOVE/RELATIONSHIPS — *Virgo*

If you do not have a partner, do not criticize yourself. You may be too self-critical. It is also possible that potential partners may seem to be overly critical of you, of other people, unable to handle criticism, or a confusing mixture of all these things.

Problems with partners may also be a result of your attitude toward criticism. Whether you are in a relationship or not, fear of criticism can lead you to search out a younger, simpler, less successful, or less educated person who would be less likely to criticize you. This may work out, but could prove disastrous later if your partner learned how to criticize from watching you. Criticism is a tool; like a hammer, it can be used to build or destroy. Criticism can become a habit, so look inside yourself to see if this is true for you or your partner. If it is, stop it as best you can. If you use your critical ability with a conscious intent to help your partner or a potential partner, keeping in mind that the justness of your criticism must be tempered with the mercy of your mutual love, you will build your loving relationship on the firmest of foundations.

If you decide you can only be satisfied with a particular outcome, you will soon find yourself paralyzed with fear and worrying that things are going to go badly for you. If you become aware that you are worrying or being a perfectionist, remind yourself how many of your past worries were for nothing and that you can handle anything. A lot of seemingly trivial issues about health, food, cleanliness, being of service, and work are going to have an important impact on your relationships now. Worrying or being attached to a particular outcome will not help. Remember that peace begins when your expectations end.

WORK/CAREER — *Virgo*

Now is the time to work hard at what you do and not focus on your overall career. At this time, big career plans and ideas for expansion are not as important as taking care of the details of everything you are involved with at work. Every little job or project that you are involved with now can become important to your overall career, but you cannot tell which one. So be a bit of a perfectionist now, giving your attention to seemingly small matters.

Even pleasantries and minor rules and regulations that might ordinarily be ignored can become very important now. The precise meanings of words used in speech and writing, and the interpretation of policies are areas where you should pay close attention. It is a time to take nothing for granted.

There is nothing to be ashamed of by taking care of the little things that make the big things work. Attend to those small but critical details and, as you do so, realize that the importance of things is not always apparent in their size or attractiveness. Attending to details can often lead to worry because there seems to be almost too much to be able to deal with. Remember how many times your worries have been for nothing. Many of your present worries are most likely for nothing now.

It is an excellent time for work requiring your ability to break things down into their component parts and analyze them. Healthcare, chemistry, pharmacology, engineering, and architectural design details come to mind immediately but there are many other careers where your precise manner and keen eye will benefit you. Quality control is especially good. All arts that require masterful eye-hand coordination will provide much pleasure.

WEALTH/SUCCESS — *Virgo*

At this time, avoid worrying about what you think you lack. Even if you are in dire straights, worrying will not help you now. Concentrate on staying positive and being open to new possibilities and opportunities. If you worry, you will not see your path to wealth and success clearly. This is a time when little things can be very important. Subtle hints of how to behave and where to go are easily overwhelmed by worrying about impending problems that may or may not actually come into being.

We each bring into our life experiences to teach us the lessons we would like to learn. Some want to learn from having and others from not having. It is up to you to decide what you can learn from your present experience. If you spend your precious time thinking about what you do not have, you are wasting time that could otherwise be spent helping you increase your wealth and standing.

Worry is based on our attachment to wanting to know how things will turn out. The way to balance worry is to first acknowledge that it is based on our natural desire to avoid pain. Worry is like a well-meaning friend who keeps picking everything apart to try to make it better, yet if allowed to go on and on, what he ends up with is a pile of picked-apart pieces of a whole that does not work anymore.

Let worry have its say and thank it for its trouble. In this way, worries are allowed to serve their legitimate purpose and you will not feel bad every time you notice you are worrying. Contests related to food, health, and hygiene would be of particular benefit now. Volunteer work would also lead you to unexpected benefit. Try to be in the moment by practicing meditation, breathing, and mindfulness.

♎ LIBRA

Libra is the only sign whose symbol is not alive, not a human, animal, or fish. Its symbol is the old-fashioned balance scale, the symbol of equal measure and justice. In the Northern Hemisphere, the time of Libra is when the harvest is brought in, weighed, and measured against other years and other farmers. Perhaps this is why Libras are such an interesting mixture of refined judgment and fierce competitiveness.

Libras are very partner oriented and often find it difficult to function efficiently without one. It's not that they depend upon their partner for much. Libras need a partner so they can find out what they, themselves, think about something by bouncing it off of another person. When they find a partner who, in this way, enables them to feel the way they want to feel, they seek to make the partnership permanent. This often leads to partnerships which others have difficulty understanding. It also make Libras very concerned with living up to the conditions of partnerships. This is the origin of contracts and the law itself, and explains why Libras are often found in professions concerned with ensuring the correctness of people's behavior.

Libras will work very hard to attain the goal of resolving conflict, either through compromise and diplomacy or by fighting the good fight if they are forced to. They are constantly trying to balance the scales of Justice regarding practically everything, and that can be very trying, not only on oneself but also on those around them. Their desire to make the perfect decision can sometimes prevent them from acting decisively until it is too late to do so.

The lesson for all Libras to learn is that there is an important reason why their judgment is not as refined, elegant, and accurate as they would like it to be. They have come into this world with the astrological sign Libra because they want to learn how to develop their judgment and become the best competitors for the finer things in life. Libras hate anything they consider not up to their standards and only want to be surrounded by the best.

Librans too often allow themselves to be persuaded to abandon their own judgments and distrust their intuitions. It is like they allow the scales to be put out of balance just because they cannot believe they have arrived at a perfect solution, a solution coming from within themselves. Many Librans are constantly seeking advice, but then they waver uncertainly between an instinctive faith in their own opinions and a fear that disaster awaits them unless they follow the advice of someone else. If they lose confidence in their own views and try and reconcile them with what others may think, they can become confused, vulnerable, and aggressive.

Librans must avoid letting their tendency to look for the equal correctness of the opposite of what they are being told influence them too strongly as they receive guidance from *The Enchanted Astrologer*. They will gain no points for coming up with an argument to the information being offered. This is not a contest between what they think and what this book says. They have to suspend their tendency to argue with what they are being told.

The scales that symbolize Libra are a non-human device intended to indicate the relative weight or value of everything by attaining a position of rest, resolution, and harmony. A scale never brought to a state of equilibrium is almost worthless. Librans have a natural affinity with the unseen, intuitive side of life. With the exceedingly rare and keen perception characteristic of the sign Libra, there is no human attainment beyond their grasp.

LOVE/RELATIONSHIPS — *Libra*

You have selected one of the most positive cards of *The Enchanted Astrologer* for relationships, both romantic and committed partnerships of all kinds. If you are in a relationship, then you should continue to act as you have been. You are on the right path. Likewise, if you are not in a relationship but would like to be, continue doing what you have been doing. A relationship is right around you and you do not have to change your life in any way to bring it into your life. It will occur naturally.

Any problems you are having in finding or maintaining a relationship can be traced back to your inability to see that you have a tendency to first idealize your partner and then to feel let down when you realize that your partner is human, just like you. In order for you to bring the right kind of relationship into your life, make the necessary changes in your attitude toward your partner and toward partnership in general. There are no perfect people or perfect partnerships.

If you are without a partner, blindly devoting yourself to finding someone who must measure up to the ideal person you have in your mind will cause you to miss opportunities to meet truly wonderful people. Like you, they are not as good as they are going to be one day, but they have potential. If you insist that they be so rich, charming, good looking, or any one of a dozen other conditions, you must face the fact that you may not be the person such a perfect person would be interested in. If you are more realistic in your expectations, you are more likely to be attractive to another realistic person, the kind of person who would be good for you.

WORK/CAREER — *Libra*

At this time, it is especially beneficial for you to be working in any profession where your success depends on your ability to interact well with others. This is not the time to go it alone or to try to stand out. It is time to be a team player. A group effort is actually the best way for you to advance your individual interests now.

Your ability to size up a situation can now help you do well as a professional buyer, appraiser, or salesperson. Working in the worlds of fashion or jewelry would provide you with much success and pleasure. Interior decoration or being somehow involved in the beautification of the world would be a particularly good use of your ability to work with others, as would a job involving the law, especially contracts. Whatever job you are in now, be the one who seeks harmony and beauty and to form partnerships, even with competitors.

If you cannot get over feeling impatient with the pace of others or with the speed of your career's advancement, then try to hide it. At this time in your career, you do not have to prove that you are a unique individual. That time may come later. Your work is being appreciated, however.

There are those around you who are not so comfortable stating their opinions. For them to act so forcefully would require them to be either egotistically sure of their opinion or angry enough not to care what you thought. Consider that this may be how they think you feel toward them.

Of course, not everyone thinks this way about you. If someone in a position to do you some good is confused by your actions, then you must help him to see that you do not want his job...even if you are not sure that you do not want his job!

WEALTH/SUCCESS — *Libra*

This is a time for balancing the scales of justice so you can expect to receive compensation that has been owed you for a while. If you are involved or planning to get involved in any legal proceedings, they can be expected to conclude in your favor. It is a good time to enter into contracts that you have researched thoroughly. It is also a good time to remind all who have yet to fulfill their commitments that it is time they do so. Follow up on deals and agreements.

If you have been thinking about getting married, now is one of the best times for the two of you to make that commitment and plan the wedding. Although many people feel that getting married is one of the hardest parts of being married, this is one of those times when you will be able to deal with all of the details of the celebration. Partnerships are favored financially.

If you are now married, now is the perfect time to take a second honeymoon, even if it is only a day trip. Celebrating your relationship will benefit you more then the loss of any money or time spent. Give thanks for all that you have together.

If you are without a relationship at this time, take heart. This is one of those times when the person you have longed for is about to enter your life. Although you should probably not be talking of marriage in the early days of your relationship, this may, in fact, be the one. You could also be going into business together.

Prizes and contests with the theme of partnership, publicity, diplomacy, harmony, and balance will be very good for you. Also, you could win recognition or awards given for beauty and beautification.

ScorpiO

Scorpio is the master detective of the zodiac. If there is something or someone Scorpios want to know about, there is nothing and no one who can prevent them from discovering the hidden truth. It is as if they feel compelled to know all the secrets just in case they need to use them or to prove how powerful they are.

When it comes to their own secrets, Scorpios are equally skilled at keeping them from others. In this way they prevent others from having power over them. They will rarely volunteer information for the same reason. Power in all its forms is one of the biggest issues for Scorpios to deal with. Most of them are powerful and know it. However, if Scorpios doubt their own power, they become so attracted to it that they are willing to do practically any-thing to get it. This can obviously put them in intense and often risky situations.

Scorpios usually keep their feelings and thoughts to them-selves, for they are too deep for mere words. However, they will not hesitate to make the perfect comment at the perfect time, espe-cially if it will deflate someone's pompous ego. Scorpios aspire to a level of purity that is hard for the other signs to even imagine. This is why they are more than willing to set straight everyone whose deeds do not measure up to their words. Scorpios are keen students of psychology and always want to know what makes peo-ple do the things they do. Compulsions and strange behavior of all kinds do not faze a Scorpio one bit; in fact, their curiosity is piqued. In undeveloped Scorpios there is a tendency to use their innate understanding of human motivations for ruthless manipulation cunningly designed to attain selfish goals.

However, most Scorpios are as fearless as their most well known symbol, the scorpion. But like a scorpion, they can be so intent on stinging something that they end up stinging themselves. Their intensity is such that other people can't believe that they real-ly mean what they are saying. Scorpios are often misunderstood because of the intensity of their passion.

Scorpio has another, lesser-known symbol, the eagle and the snake. The eagle flies higher than any bird and the snake is the crea-ture lowest to the ground. This is because Scorpio is associated with the extremes of the both the highest and the lowest existing at the same time. For example, Scorpio is the sign associated with sexual reproduction, a function that is accomplished using organs of the body also used for elimination of its liquid waste products.

The lesson for Scorpios to learn is that there is an important reason why their life does not provide them with as many peak experiences as they would like. They have come into this world with the astrological sign Scorpio because they want to learn how to develop their ability to work their powerful will on the world. The sign Scorpio rules magic and they want to make big changes in their lives, the kinds that appear to other people as almost magical transformations.

When Scorpios focus their energies on controlling others, they find in the end that it is they, themselves, who end up being under the control of others. However, when they turn their efforts towards self-control, the influence they have on both others and the world around them seems to be without bounds. It is as if the best way for them to control a situation is to be in control of themselves.

Scorpios must avoid their tendency to test their answers from *The Enchanted Astrologer* against the most extreme of hypothetical circumstances. That can distract them from listening to information that can help them become more powerful.

LOVE/RELATIONSHIPS — *Scorpio*

Expect passion and intensity in your relationships now. This is not the time for half measures. Although your life may take on the appearance of a romance novel, this is as it should be. Relationships that you thought were over and done with may resurrect themselves. A relationship that has been built on anything other than truth may end. The use and exchange of power can either make or break a relationship now.

Do not reveal secrets to anyone if you want to keep them secret. Do not volunteer information that you have not been asked for, and even then, you should consider every word you say. You may be made aware that certain people have been telling you half-truths. You are a great detective now and if you suspect someone of this, it would be easy for you to investigate the matter.

People often rush into having a sexual relationship before they have any other kind of basis for their being together. This is not only dangerous, but it is often the result of a desire for approval. You do not need the approval of others to feel good about yourself. Feeling empty inside can also be a motivation for rushing into the sexual aspect of a loving relationship before it is time to do so. When you feel empty, you are willing to settle for any experience that feels important. In this way, you feel alive.

Choose a partner you like and who is willing to wait a while before moving your relationship to the physical stage. When you find that person, you can rest assured that a wonderful time in your life is at hand. Resisting your sexual urges is not an easy thing to do sometimes, but it is very important that you do so now.

WORK/CAREER — *Scorpio*

You may decide to end a job or an aspect of your career that is obviously not working for you. If so, cut your losses and move on with confidence; the change will do you good.

Issues of power, control, and secrecy are all important now. Keep secrets and do not volunteer information, even about the most trivial of things. Pretend that you are on a secret mission. In a very real way, you are. When the time is right you will be part of a major change for the better, one that may be quite sweeping in nature. When that happens, you will be able to enjoy your new and successful career move with anyone and everyone.

The necessity for secrecy may cause you to act like you know something others do not. Others may misunderstand you and your motives now. However, for now, do not reveal the secret of what you are doing to anyone, even those you are positive will support you in your new enterprise. The ability to keep knowledge away from those not ready to hear it is as important as gaining the knowledge yourself. Avoid the temptation to manipulate people in the belief that your goal justifies any means possible. This would create repercussions that would prevent your dream from coming true in the near future. However, with a little forethought, this potential impediment is easily avoided.

It is a time for the resurrection of an aspect of your work or career plan you thought was dead and buried. It will not come back the way you thought it would, but it will come back to life. If you are between jobs now, consider doing a type of work that you have not done for a long time. Jobs with a Scorpio flavor are detective work, recycling, power management, managing other people's resources and careers, banking, acting as an agent, magic, and everything involved with sexuality.

Wealth/Success — *Scorpio*

You can increase your wealth by using and managing other people's resources now. It is just as important that you manage it honestly as successfully. A project or investment you may have given up for dead may now come back to life. Don't be surprised to see yourself making things appear and disappear as if by magic. You are very powerful now and can influence others with your magnetic personality.

There is also the likelihood that you are going to be approached with a get-rich-quick scheme. If it looks too good to be true, it probably is. Check into the secret details of any financial dealings you become involved with, for this is also a time of secrecy. Keep your plans secret and do not volunteer information unless you have to. If someone confides in you, keep his or her confidence.

If you are involved with children, it is a good time to protect them from seeing, hearing, and experiencing things beyond their years. Be aware that they may be holding some secrets from you at this time. Most are probably the innocent secrets of childhood learning experiences. Make sure that they know you are interested in them and that you will believe what they tell you. It is important that they know you are on their side. If not, they may believe someone else has their best interests at heart when, in fact, they do not.

This is a good time to receive awards or enter contests where your ability to discover or even just plain guess secrets wins you a prize. You should be able to win something if it has a magical, mystical, or detective theme about it. This is also a time for receiving gifts from others in the form of grants, scholarships, and inheritances. It is a very good time to plan your estate or set up a trust fund.

SAGITTARIUS

The symbol for Sagittarius is Chiron, the bow-wielding Centaur —half-man and half-horse. Chiron the Centaur was the first doctor of herbal medicine and a wise sage. In Greek mythology, he was the teacher of the great warrior Achilles.

The legend of Chiron may have started out with stories of a wise and skillful hunter, perhaps the leader of the first tribe to hunt from the back of a horse. The other tribes might have seen them as being half-man and half-horse. Travel on horseback made it possible for people to see many more different places and tribes with all kinds of unique customs. When they returned from their journeys, they kept their own tribe hypnotized with stories of these far off lands.

Those born under the sign of Sagittarius share this love of travel and animals – especially horses, the great outdoors, natural healing, and all things foreign. They are the philosopher teachers of the zodiac and without this vital function, each generation would be forced to start from scratch without the accumulated wisdom of the ages to guide them. Sagittarians not only keep the torch of learning alive, they actively seek out knowledge and the wisdom to use it properly. They are interested only in the ultimate truth; otherwise it would not be worth knowing and teaching to others.

This is why Sagittarians have such a reputation for being blunt. Sagittarians feel that anyone who is telling the truth should be able to defend his position against any question, even if that question is totally tactless and without regard for social customs. Sagittarians are in a hurry and want to keep traveling, learning, and spreading what they've learned. They don't have time to waste beating around the bush. Never expect them to apologize for having annoyed someone when they were only trying to get at the truth.

The lesson for Sagittarians to learn is that there is an important reason why their life does not provide them with as many opportunities to travel, to learn, and to teach, as they would like. They have come into the world with the astrological sign Sagittarius because they want to learn how to study, travel, and especially how to teach. They can use their desire and capacity to expand their understanding of the way the world works in many ways. They can use it to take them around the world, both through actual travel and through travel in their minds via philosophy and learning. Publishing and broadcasting are two other ways to bring the world to us.

When Sagittarians are required to act immediately, without having the time to think about what they are doing, they possess all the courage they need to do anything they need to do. However, when they are allowed the luxury of having enough time to think about what is required of them, they are inclined to be timid and cautious. It is important that Sagittarians not become so inspired by each new piece of wisdom they learn that they decide to put off the plans of yesterday to make yet another grand plan to change their lives, and then cancel their plans tomorrow when new information becomes available.

It is also important that Sagittarians avoid their tendency to resist taking care of the details necessary to implement any successful plan. No sign is as fearless and broad-minded as theirs when it comes to encountering the new and the strange, yet they need to develop tolerance for the necessary and the routine. Thinking big is a useful trait, but it will only take you so far.

LOVE/RELATIONSHIPS — *Sagittarius*

This is a time when you will be lucky in love. By keeping an open mind to things you might often overlook as being too strange or foreign, you will see opportunities to learn about people in a way that will make you very attractive.

You can find love in the great outdoors. Taking part in or even watching sporting events are favorable ways to find, maintain, and improve a relationship. Nature excursions would be great for you. Even if you are usually the kind of person who stays inside, go out for a walk. You have to increase your awareness of the world around you. A walk to the library would include the two best ways to expand your awareness about the world.

It is a time to be as honest and direct as you comfortably can be. Even if you have something negative to say, now is the time you will be able to do so without hurting anyone's feelings. However, if there are any bad intentions involved, you will soon identify them and take action to place yourself outside of their range of influence. Changes you make within yourself will be seen and felt as changes in your experience of the world.

You will then be making fast progress toward bringing into your life the kind of relationship where you each understand and respect each other's views, especially about the help being offered you by friends and relatives. In fact, you will bring into your life the kind of relationship where the two of you will be extremely close and loving. It will be easy for you to make boundaries between the two of you and your friends and family. More importantly, the two of you will be so obviously good for each other that no one would even think of suggesting to tell you to change things even a little.

WORK/CAREER — *Sagittarius*

It is time to improve your education and job skills, especially your management skills. You have to learn how best to delegate. It is not so much because you are falling behind current standards, but because this is such a lucky time for you that expending extra effort will seem to come back to you tenfold.

It is time to expand your mind about what is possible in this world. Either you bring the world to you through newspapers, magazines, books, television, radio, broadcasting, the Internet, wireless technologies, and other techniques for the widespread distribution of knowledge, or you take yourself to the world through travel. You would do well to seek a job in the publishing, broadcasting, Internet, and communications fields, as well as anything to do with the travel industry. Working outdoors, in sports or fitness, and with horses or other animals would be ideal.

The most obvious way to bring yourself to the world would be through work that took you outdoors or required that you travel. You might even find that you expanded your career opportunities by taking a trip.

Going hand-in-hand with expanding your perceptions about the world is a new appreciation for what the word "truth" really means. As you expand your understanding, you will realize more and more that for each person, there are many things that are true for them because of the unique position they are in. Accept this fact and you will succeed faster.

It is also extremely important that you speak the truth at all times regarding your work and your career. This concern for truth would make a career involving you with the justice system a very smart career move. It would give you an outlet for you to be able to tell the truth to all, as well as to hear the truth spoken equally bluntly to you by others.

WEALTH/SUCCESS — *Sagittarius*

This is a most fortunate time for you and you should enjoy it. Your directness and ability to think big are paying off. It is time for you to learn a lot more about the lifestyles of the famous and rich. Until now, you may have had a theoretical understanding of how it feels to have other people look at you and be slightly envious of your good fortune. Soon success and wealth will be real for you and show you the tradeoffs that are necessary when fortune smiles.

You would do well to be very generous and tolerant of others. In this way, you will gain their trust and confidence. They will protect you from any jealousy and false rumors that may follow you as a result of your good fortune. Also, your tolerant, generous, and expanded awareness will enable you to deal with any petty jealousies that may arise. Not only should you have more sympathy for and from those you might have envied at one time, but also you should extend your compassion to those who are not as fortunate as you are now. It is a time to remember your roots and to see how far you have come from where you were.

Wealth and success may now come to you through sports, everything that is natural and pure, animals (especially horses), philosophy, travel, justice, broadcasting, and publishing.

If there are children in your life, now would be an excellent time to take actions to ensure that they will have a higher education waiting for them when they are ready. Scholarships and all manner of investments designed to pay for higher education is favored now. It is time to broaden their horizons in every way possible. Giving them the means to travel would be a good way, although traveling with them would be best.

CAPRICORN

A mountain goat with a fish's tail symbolizes Capricorn. A curious symbol, to be sure, but yet it perfectly represents the dual nature of those born during the time of Capricorn. The mountain goat is tireless as it makes its way to the tops of mountain after mountain. Most Capricorns are equally tireless in their efforts to get to the top of their respective professions. Most people might think that Capricorns desire above all to attain the respect of the masses. It is more accurate to say that they crave the respect of those that they, themselves, respect. This is as important to them as living in wealth and style, yet another way they gain the respect of the in crowd.

To get to the top, Capricorns are willing to do what is expected of them. This gets them the reputation of being conservative, when deep inside, they are quite sensual. They are conservative in the best sense of the word. You conserve what you have so that you will have enough when you need it. This is true practicality. Capricorns make wonderful executives. In fact, it is difficult for them to show their true worth until they are left alone to assume some kind of definite responsibility. Once they feel this weight resting on their shoulders they will rise to the occasion, succeeding where others would give up. Once they realize that it is up to them to make something of themselves, they display a kind of energy that can overcome almost any obstacle.

Remember the fish's tail that the Capricorn mountain goat is dragging behind him? The ancients use the element water to symbolize emotion and the tail is used by fish to propel and steer themselves in their watery world. Capricorn people have very deep and real emotional needs that can slow them down considerably or even stop them in their tracks.

The lesson for Capricorns centers on the important reason why their life does not provide them with as many opportunities to enjoy success, wealth, and happiness, as they would like. They have come into this world with the astrological sign Capricorn because they want to learn the best way to achieve success, wealth, and happiness. They know in their hearts that there are actual techniques they need to learn and lessons they need to apply in their lives before they can attain their full potential.

Their awareness of how far they have to go to achieve the respect they crave can sometimes get to them and make them pessimistic or, less often, depressed. This tendency actually comes not from the realization of how far they have to go, but from the fact that they will rarely allow themselves to become inspired and energized by what they have already accomplished. Though they may not see it as well as those around them, they have, from a young age, already accomplished many things that would be sufficient to delight those who are not Capricorns. Further contributing to their tendency towards depression are the pressures caused by their desire to maintain a prosperous appearance, keeping pace with both fashion and tradition, while at the same time living in luxury and ease and, in some way, above the level of the masses whose praises they seek.

When Capricorns start on the road to success, their persistence and ability to focus on a goal enables them to succeed and to become authority figures in their chosen field. If they can do what has to be done and maintain a sense of humor to help them get through the difficult times, they are unstoppable.

LOVE/RELATIONSHIPS — *Capricorn*

At this time, love and relationships are wrapped up with you or your partner's work and career. If you or your partner is not doing well in those areas, there will be problems in your relationships. Rich or poor, if you, your partner, or both of you are not working or enjoying the same level of success or career satisfaction, your relationship will suffer. Also, if either or both of you are not doing what you know you should be doing with your life, this will be a source of irritation to either or both of you and may even lead to depression.

If you are in a committed relationship, you can strengthen it by having your partner understand your work problems and support you in your efforts to better your position. If your partner is not supportive of your career now, it will cause great stress on you and your relationship. This might be a good time to investigate working together with your romantic partner in some practical way. You might work together at your existing jobs or start a new business altogether. Do not quit your job until you are certain beyond a doubt that any new business could support you both.

If you are not in a committed relationship, then one is most likely come to you now during your work hours. It could come at your place of employment, but not necessarily. Partners now could tend to be older than you might usually be interested in. There would be an element of teacher and student that you would enjoy.

Now is a time when you need the respect of those you consider important in your life. It is not the time to risk your reputation in any way. If you have worked hard and built a great relationship, you will be recognized for your achievement now.

Work/Career — *Capricorn*

It is a great time to focus on your career goals even more than on your everyday job. You can advance yourself now better than almost any other time. The reason you are being asked to work so hard is so that you can enjoy all the rewards that come to you later. You will enjoy them even more if you postpone any but the most essential pleasure trips for a while and concentrate on the advancement of your career. It is necessary for you to delay many immediate sources of gratification such as social engagements and recreational activities in favor of things directly connected with your career.

You will soon be given the opportunity to show how worthy of promotion you are. You are being tested to see if you should be able to join the club of those who are richer and more powerful than you. At some time in the near or distant past they were in your position and now they want to help someone like you. Help them decide that it is you they should be helping.

It is more important that you show them how similar you are to them in every way than how different you are. It is important for you to reassure those in a position to help you that you approve of them and would like to learn what they know and do what they do. Save any ideas you have for the reforming of a situation for a time when you have successfully established yourself and are in a position to use your power to really make a difference. Right now, the best thing you can do is take a deep breath and allow success to carry you along like a log in a swiftly flowing river. Do not try to push the river where you want it to go.

Wealth/Success — *Capricorn*

Everything connected with your career is likely to benefit you greatly now. Promotions, sales, raises, bonuses, business loans, and even business gifts are all coming your way now. Long-term investments can pay off now and your long-term goals reached. Make every effort not to be late for a while. You will come across an opportunity for recognition you would have missed had you been late.

Contests and awards where you can be recognized for your accomplishments are favored more highly than those of a pure chance nature. Company sponsored contests or awards for the attaining of sales goals are more likely to go to you than to others. Well-known and established contests are also favored, as are prizes given to those who display excellent timing.

If there are children in your life, this is a good time to teach them the importance of respecting themselves and others for both their inner strength and their outer achievements. You may have to be a bit stern with them now for this is not a time for joking around. It is a time for them to learn that there is a time for everything, even being serious about their efforts to attain wealth and success. One of the unfortunate consequences of the instant TV/movie generation is that they see the story of successful people presented in a couple of hours or less. They have no idea how much dedication, work, rejection, disappointment, and self-motivation is necessary for a human being to build a successful life. This is the perfect time to teach them what you know about the value of planning and patience. They will listen to someone like you, a person who will have gained the respect of those in their immediate circle and maybe even beyond.

The symbol of the sign Aquarius is the Water bearer pouring out his bounty to quench the thirst of world. For this reason, many people mistakenly think Aquarius is a water sign. Water was the element the ancient sages connected with the realm of emotion, empathy, and intuition. However, Aquarius is not a water sign. The element associated with Aquarius is Air, the realm of ideas. People born under the sign Aquarius like to think in broad and theoretical terms and they want to "pour out" their ideas to quench the thirst of the world.

Being mistaken for a water sign is a very significant clue to the lesson for Aquarians. Water symbolizes emotions and empathy and Aquarians are often perceived to be lacking in both.

Aquarians, being concerned for the good of all, are inspired to invent solutions to society's problems. They are the mad scientists and absent-minded professors of the zodiac. To do this requires a freethinking mind, unfettered by tradition or fear of disturbing the status quo. Aquarians learn from the past to change what they find distasteful in the present, for by doing so they create the future they envision. The emotional detachment necessary to clearly see society's problems and to try to solve those problems without regard to the ramifications of the actions necessary to make these sometimes drastic changes make Aquarians seem to lack empathy for the hardships of individuals. Aquarians should examine actions they plan to take to make sure they will not be hurtful to others, even if that is not their intent.

Once the scientific minds of Aquarians finish thinking about a subject theoretically, they return to the world of emotions. In fact, they can easily feel themselves being overcome by feelings of empathy for those less fortunate. This is what inspires them in the first place to come up with solutions to society's urgent problems. This brings us to the basic lessons all Aquarians would do well to keep in mind as they read the meanings of card they draw from *The Enchanted Astrologer*'s deck.

A baby does not arrive in the world already an expert in the things his astrological sign is known for. Aquarians are here to learn how to invent ways to make real the future they can so easily see in their minds' eye. This is the reason why their lives do not provide them with as many opportunities to enjoy the freedom and other resources necessary to turn their innovative ideas into reality as they would like.

When Aquarians finally become convinced that they must stop dreaming about the kind of future they would like to live in and start working to make it a reality, they can be counted on to work until their goals are achieved. In fact, they sometimes make such extreme changes that in their enthusiasm to get rid of the old ways, they can destroy valuable things from the past that still have great usefulness. The old expression for this is "Throwing out the baby with the bathwater."

If Aquarians want to have the kind of lives they have always dreamed of having, they must avoid letting their tendency to go to extremes cause them to imagine that they must make radical changes in their lives that are really too much to ask of themselves and others, changes that are bound to be too difficult to maintain. People do not usually have to make sweeping, radical changes in their lives to bring in the love, wealth, and success that they desire, especially the kind of extreme changes that Aquarians would be willing to make without a second's thought.

LOVE/RELATIONSHIPS — *Aquarius*

If you do not have a relationship now, a current friendship may soon blossom into one. You may also find love through a friend's help. In existing relationships, it is very important that you treat each other with the kind of loving forgiveness and understanding that many people reserve just for their best friends. A relationship without friendship is in danger of failing now.

At the heart of any present problems or questions you have now regarding your love life may be the fact that you or your partner is afraid that the next stage in the development of your relationship will require one or both of you to give up your own life with your own hopes, dreams and desires. So you resist doing what you know you must do to bring your relationship to the next level and it is getting stale. If you do not have a loving relationship in your life, you may fear that doing so will require you to give up your independence and an exciting life, when you never know what is going to happen next.

It may be true that in the past your experience of the word "love" caused you to feel smothered and imprisoned by what you thought was love. You may have felt confused about yourself and your own needs and so you could have become attracted to someone whose own needs were obvious and required immediate attention. In this way you gave up on your own hopes and dreams and devoted yourself to helping your partner accomplish his.

That is not an option for you now. You must become yourself as fully as possible now. It is time to invent a way for you to have a relationship that you can live with. It may not be conventional in any way, but it will be a unique statement of your individuality.

WORK/CAREER — *Aquarius*

Now is a good time to profit from an invention or original idea. Also, work that allows you to do things that you find new and exciting will do well for you in both the long and short term. It is time for you to become comfortable with the unexpected; include it in your planning. You will learn that it can be a pleasant experience. There are lots of wonderful surprises coming your way so do your best to bring newness into your life.

By being too set in your ways you have created a situation that requires you to break out of your rut now. The minute you even begin to think about being open to new ways of doing things, you will begin to see some of the possibilities for change that are around you at this time. It will be like taking the first breath of spring air; when you feel that marvelous feeling, you will know that career improvement is on the way.

Take the time to correct your course of action a little bit now. Like priming a pump, it is necessary for you to bring the first few small changes for the better into your life. Do not get stuck in wanting things to turn out one way to the exclusion of all other ways. It is important for you to be open to changing your plans to suit the present situation.

You might find it beneficial to volunteer for the things you might have resisted volunteering for in the past. Now is the time to put yourself in a position where opportunity can find you. A job that involves more travel or exposure to new inventions or unusual situations would really get your career flowing. The many changes you are going to experience are ushering in one of the most exciting and rewarding times in your life.

Wealth/Success — *Aquarius*

You need to "re-invent" yourself in some way. Making new friends will benefit you now. You will be able to look at yourself thorough the eyes of someone who does not know you well. You will be able to put your best foot forward and get a chance to examine what it is that you consider important now. Think "outside of the box" and you will find new ways to increase your prosperity.

Wealth and success are likely to come your way through clubs and fraternal associations. Interact with those who share a common interest with you. Listen to any advice they want to give you about realizing your dreams and reaching your potential, even if it seems eccentric or downright crazy.

Any award or contest whose payout was stretched out into the future would do well for you. Those with an astrological connection or something to do with numerology, the science of numbers, would also be favored. Also, any games and prizes with a scientific, space, futuristic or historic theme would attract your interest and be more likely to pay off for you.

If there are children in your life this is a good time to show them there is a bit of the genius or eccentric in you. If you have been noticing a child getting too wrapped up in her personal life, now would be a good time to expose her to humanitarian goals. More importantly, it would be a time to show her how humanitarian goals are reached by interacting with individual people, not by looking at humanity as something separate from the human beings who do not usually follow any plan, no matter how elegant. It is a time for you to teach and learn, on a new level, the importance of looking at each situation as if you have seen it for the first time.

♓ Pisces

Pisces is the last sign of the zodiac. Because it is the last of the twelve signs, it contains a bit of all of them. This is one explanation of why Pisces people are so easily able to understand how other people are feeling. In fact, Pisceans are so sensitive to the feelings of others that it is not good for them to be near people who are angry, sad, or disturbed. Sometimes, it is hard for those born during the time of Pisces to understand why they are feeling the way they are. If they take the time to investigate a little, they often realize that they are literally picking up on the feelings of others.

Pisces is associated with both empathy and telepathy. This natural ability to be invisibly connected to those around them and those around the world is both the blessing and the curse of all Pisceans. It enables them to feel exactly how to help those they care about, which is a Piscean specialty. It also exhausting and hard on a Piscean person's emotions to have other people's lives intrude so on their own.

Sometimes, naturally, there is a strong desire to escape from doing the double duty of experiencing both their own emotions and the emotions of those around them. This is why Pisceans often develop a means to escape from their sensitiveness. No sign is as good at creating their own fantasy world, either through writing and the visual arts, through mood-altering substances, or through making enough money to make their world as isolated and comfortable as possible. They get into trouble when they use drugs, alcohol, sex, gambling, religious zealotries, and any other escape devices that overwhelm their common sense and senses, and block out the real world.

When they turn their sensitivity to the real world, Pisceans have the capacity to make incredible amounts of money in business ventures. If you think that seems unlikely given Pisces' reputation for dreaminess and escapism, remember that as the last sign, Pisces contains a bit of all the other signs. They have the ability to achieve an overview of any business situation and their sensitivity to others enables them to know how others will feel and act. That enables them to make accurate predictions that tell them how to act to reap the greatest rewards.

The lesson for Pisces centers on the important reason why their lives do not provide them with as many opportunities to use their unique sensitivity to others to gain the appreciation and respect of those they would most like to help and associate with. They have come into this world born under the astrological sign Pisces because they want to learn how to get close enough to people to be of assistance to them, yet without becoming overwhelmed by their needs and actions.

The more honest and honorable Pisceans are, the more they hesitate. They seem to fear that they may not be able to fulfill their promises, or that the world will expect more of them than they can give.

Pisceans are most aware of both the things that unite us all and the immense differences between people. This is one of their great strengths, but if they let themselves be totally ruled by their emotions or let the sorrow of the human condition push them to escapist behavior, it can turn into a great weakness. When they learn to balance their innate intuitive skills with a logical approach that does not ignore what is real but unpleasant, they can accomplish great things.

LOVE/RELATIONSHIPS — *Pisces*

Relationships where you shared a passion for religious, spiritual, intuitive, or even psychic phenomena would benefit you now. If you are not in a relationship, then attending events related to these things would most probably lead to you to one.

Be very careful not to escape into a world of your own now. The desire to experience other worlds and spiritual union should not keep you from fulfilling your practical obligations. Escape through the use of drugs, alcohol, or any other addictions must be avoided at all costs now. They are usually used to shut out our reality, but it is only through facing reality that we can grow.

All too often, denial is used as a way of avoiding an unpleasant present reality. Many people would rather convince themselves that they are in a fine relationship, but one that is actually doing them no good, rather than admit their problems. If they did admit how hurt and angry it made them, they would have to either admit that they were too afraid to do something or too afraid to get out of the relationship. It is surprising how many people will resist facing up to their responsibilities, even when children are involved.

But children or no, even the most spiritual and powerful force in the universe, forgiveness, may be being used as a disguise for denial and weakness. If there is alcohol, drugs, abuse, violence, or adultery standing between you and the truly loving relationship you dream of, you cannot deny or condone these dangerous and destructive forces forever. If this is the case, you must face what is happening and take immediate steps to correct the problem. If the damaged person will not do what is neccessary, then you should do everything you can to get out of the situation. You can forgive at a distance, too.

WORK/CAREER — *Pisces*

No matter what job you find yourself doing at the present time, you can reap great rewards by being sensitive to the needs of others. It may appear that you are giving more than you are getting in return but that is just the way things appear on the surface. Helping others who are deserving of your help is one of the surest ways of bringing good fortune to everything you do.

It is crucial that you feel emotionally fulfilled by your work. If it were too coarse or hurtful to others, such work would sometimes make you feel upset or physically ill. If you are forced to be around people who are very emotionally unstable, mean, or negative, you might feel yourself taking on these emotions when you least wanted to. Shield yourself from these people's presence by visualizing that a suit of armor made from pure white light protects you.

Any work or career that stifles your feelings must be eliminated, if possible. Of course, it is equally important that you do not upset yourself or others in your attempt to breathe new energy into your emotional life. When you make the first attempts to re-connect with your feelings and intuitions, you may find all kinds of feelings flooding over you. It is this uncontrollable aspect of our emotions and intuitions that makes many people uncomfortable with them. This may very well be the reason you thought it necessary to detach yourself from your emotions.

Without going overboard, you may find that you can assist those less fortunate than you. It is important that you first make sure the people and causes you are serving are truly deserving of your assistance; if you feel that they are, go ahead and do what you can.

Wealth/Success — *Pisces*

The wealth and success coming up for you now may be manifesting themselves in a spiritual way. Spirituality is derived from the fact that when we go looking for who we really are, we find that to a large degree we are not our bodies, but we are our spirit. Our spirit is our true wealth and cannot be taken away from us. We can, however, forget our spirit and its power in our lives.

As spiritual beings, we are able to visualize what we believe to be true, or what we want to be true, and then materialize our spiritual vision in reality. That may seem like an unrealistic view of how the world works, but realize that everything around you was first an idea in someone's mind. We can visualize wealth and success all we want, but we will have more luck if we put our heart and mind and our body into the equation, too. If we think that there is something unspiritual about having money, then we will never allow our spirit to help us have the abundance that is our birthright. We must always remember that we have power over our reality through our thoughts and our willpower. Our willpower is stronger than our bad habits.

If there are children in your life, now is a good time to show them the value of working for a cause greater than themselves. It is a time to show them the practical value of a charitable attitude. Children under the age of seven would really benefit from such gentle teaching, for the world they know is closest to this loving and openhearted spirituality. By interacting with them, you will see ways for you to return to the quiet strength that this type of childlike faith can give.

MARS

Mars is the planet that represents our strength, our will, and our ability to go get what we want. It represents the Male principle, i.e., needing to take action to make things the way you want them to be. When the energies of Mars are blocked or misdirected, they often burst through in the form of impatience, hostility, and sometimes violence. Mars was the god of war in Roman times when war was considered an almost ideal way to develop an individual's strength of mind, body, and character, as well as the strength of the whole nation. At least, that is what their leaders wanted men to think. Today, the war we are challenged to fight is no less challenging. The information overload, chaos, and frenzied pace of everyday life demands that we use our Mars energies to work our will on the world. That takes the strength of character and the focused willpower of Mars.

LOVE/RELATIONSHIPS — *Mars*

If you do not have a partner, one may come into your life soon in a very bold way. He or she may just come right up to you and get the relationship going, or it may be you who overcomes the fear of rejection and acts directly and decisively.

You must be the assertive one in your relationships now, even if you are not usually that kind of person. Do not wait for anyone or anything. Respond quickly to anyone who contradicts you. Allow yourself to act on your first impulse and do not second-guess yourself. Feel the rightness of your cause.

Take control of your life. Any lack of control, especially self-control, is manifesting as a frustrating inability to make things go the way you want them to. Just keep in mind that you may be thought to be selfish by other people when you do. This is practically unavoidable now, but you must not let that stop you. Think of yourself as a warrior and stop being a worrier, especially about what other people think.

In rare cases, picking this card when asking about love and relationships can be a warning to avoid dangerous or abusive behavior at all costs. It is much more likely that it indicates that some time in the near or distant past, one of you put too much emphasis on control and spent your time either trying to control others or resenting the fact that others had the power of control in their hands. Whether you resisted this manipulation or surrendered your power, or especially if you are still in the grip of such a situation, the problem is that one or both of you may be judging yourselves too harshly. It is important that you start to develop healthy self-esteem now. Use the power of affirmations to reinforce your goals.

WORK/CAREER — *Mars*

An original spark of an idea regarding the advancement of your career will soon come into your mind. Do not blow out this spark with fear or self-doubt, but allow it to burn brightly for all to see. Act on this impulse without second-guessing yourself. Show everyone how strong you are and how strong your willpower is. Your career is going to advance more quickly than you thought, whether or not it looks that way now.

Do not stop your advance by adding your own self-critical voice to those with less than your best interests at heart. Be brave and let others criticize or work against you all they want. Show everyone that you are a warrior, not a worrier. Be confident and draw strength from the knowledge that you have taken action and will conduct yourself correctly. The challenges that come your way now are opportunities to show who you are to those in authority. They know what it's like to want career advancement. It is better to work in a position where your efforts can be seen by those with the power to help you.

You are working on your ability to anticipate what must be done and then to do it without being told what to do. Demonstrating this skill with honesty, bravery, and willpower will lead to advances in your career. Having a self-motivated problem solver like you around is worth its weight in gold. If you balance your desire to advance your career by showing others that you desire to help your team succeed, then your recognition is assured.

If you are without a job or want to change jobs, you will do well to seek one where you can demonstrate your strength of mind, body, willpower or all three.

WEALTH/SUCCESS — *Mars*

You cannot get what you want until you are sure of what you want. Draw up a list of your goals and desires so as to crystallize them in your mind. Let them come to you spontaneously. Do not censor yourself. You will be surprised at what rises to the surface of your consciousness. Follow it with a list of what you are going to do when your goals are attained. This will help you clarify and define your original list of goals.

Do not look back on past failures with regret. Draw strength from your accomplishments. If you are not failing, you are not trying. Successful people fail, too, but they keep trying and trying at so many things that their failures appear to be steps on the path to success, not walls that keep them from their goals. Look at your accomplishments the way your best friend would. Do not denigrate them just because they were not achieved in some impossibly perfect way.

Trust that you have the power to take control of your own life. Your decisions and actions have brought you to where you are and it is your decisions and your actions that are going to bring you to where you want to go. You have the power to create the circumstances that you experience. When you do what you know you must do to get where you want to go, you will be able to enjoy the kind of life you have been dreaming of that much sooner.

If you are fortunate enough to be sound enough in mind and body to be able to do so, appreciate the wealth of being clear-headed enough to be able to think for yourself and for the ability to act without assistance.

P
L
A
N
E
T
S

NORTH NODE

The North Node is not a planet; it is an ever-changing point of intersection between the moving paths of the Moon and the Earth. Its symbol shows the two planets connected by a shared path and that path is pointed north. The North Node symbolizes the best way our inner emotional life can help us succeed with our long-term goals. If we are not emotionally fulfilled inside of ourselves, no amount of outward love or success will make us feel good about the world or ourselves. The North Node symbolizes being in harmony with what we should be doing to reach the place in our lives we have decided will make us feel emotionally fulfilled. It is the method by which we can shake off any ill feelings about our past actions and be reborn. Picking the North Node is a sign that you are on the right track to the fulfillment of your destiny.

LOVE/RELATIONSHIPS — *North Node*

If you do not have a relationship, you may soon be experiencing real love. Love can change your life as nothing else can. It is the best thing life can offer. True love is when you enjoy just being with your partner, watching her live, and wanting only to help her live her dream. This is different from the thrill of romance, but much better, more important, and long lasting. Even if this true love doesn't seem to be returned by the object of your affections now, the fact that you know what love is will lead you to either getting it returned from your present love interest or finding someone else who will love you the way you know you should be loved.

If you do have a partner, then you or your partner, or both of you are on the right track toward the fulfillment of your dreams. Even if it does not seem like that now, you are doing what you should be doing to make your relationship all it can be. Do not change your course, unless there is physical, emotional, or mental abuse or any other destructive activity involved in your relationship.

Accept your good fortune. You will soon realize that you can be loved and cherished for every aspect of your personality. You will discover wonderful aspects of life you would have otherwise missed. The passion you now feel or will soon feel can last and extend into every aspect of your life.

If your relationship is new, make sure your partner is someone whom you like a lot and who is willing to wait awhile before moving your relationship to the physical stage. When you find that person, you can rest assured that a wonderful time in your life is at hand and that the fabulous love life you will come to know will be with someone positive whom you love and trust.

P
L
A
N
E
T
S

WORK/CAREER — *North Node*

You are in very good position to advance your career. You will soon be absolutely clear about what you need to move to the next stage of your career and once you know that, you will be able to get it. You have gotten the attention of those who can help you. They may not be applauding you but they are watching. You are looked on a lot more favorably than you might think. They fear to be seen as showing favoritism to you so they do not show how much they think of you.

Now is one of the best times for insuring the advancement of your career goals. Whether you are looking for more money, a better title, or work that you think you would enjoy more, you are about to be asked to do something that will lead to all that and more. Stay alert. Reward may not come in the form you are looking for. It is up to you to be able to read the situation correctly.

Now, it is up to you to show them that you are smart enough to be aware of what is not working for you in your career and to fix it. They know how hard it is for them to cope with their own faults, so if you display a willingness to cope with your own they will be impressed. You will be surprised at how willing people are to help someone who is obviously making an effort to correct a situation they have had a part in creating. Only great people are capable of this feat.

Of course, you may encounter some who will appear not be so forgiving, but take heart. You have gotten out of your own way and are allowing your supporters to help you attain the kind of satisfying career you have always dreamed of.

WEALTH/SUCCESS — *North Node*

Your life is about to change for the better in many ways. It is almost time for you to experience gain and success in the things that matter to you. There will soon be more of the things you need to live the kind of life you want. This is the measure of true wealth and success. "Free" time is often the most expensive luxury to come by.

This is a lucky time. The good you have sewn is coming back to you. You are on the right path to wealth and success and should stick to it. Forget past disappointments and move on to this golden time in your life. You are entering an important stage, a time when you will be able to go within yourself and trust the guidance you will receive from those close to you and those you have helped in the past. You have learned many important lessons, including the most important one of all: true wealth and success is the result of sharing whatever good fortune you possess with those whom you think deserve it.

Your value system is at the heart of the good news you are soon going to hear regarding your wealth and success. Your earning ability is limited only by your beliefs. Believe that there is enough wealth in the world for you to have your fair share because this is a very lucky time for you. Ask for what you want, even from people who have said no to you in the past. Just be careful to ask for what you really want, because you will probably get it. Try to foresee the consequences of getting your wish granted in the way you want it to be. You may want to modify your wish a little.

P
L
A
N
E
T
S

MERCURY

In Greek mythology, Mercury was described as the young swift messenger of the gods with wings on his feet and helmet. In astrology Mercury is the planet of communication, the constant back and forth exchanges that are swift, and ever changing. It also rules the thought processes that produce communication, our rational mind and our ability to use logic to analyze a situation. The restless curiosity of Mercury, learning a little about practically everything, associates the planet with youth — both youthful enthusiasm and follies — and the kind of games and practical jokes played by young people. Mercury is about what you think, not what you feel or believe. It flits across the surface of life scanning, relating, and reporting back the obvious facts, not the deep underlying principles and truths. Mercury rules memory, which gives us our sense of history and of our place in time, and makes prediction possible.

Love/Relationships — *Mercury*

If you do not have a relationship, the reason may be related to how busy, smart, young, immature, quick, talkative, changeable, or superficial you or any potential partners for you are. Problems of personality are usually caused when there is either too much or too little of a particular quality.

You or the person you are interested in could be talking when you should be listening or a quiet manner may be misinterpreted as a lack of thoughtfulness or interest. One or both of you may be so busy that you do not seem to have time for anyone or so uninvolved that you annoy people. Your ages may not be appropriate or one or both of you may be acting too young or too old for your age. Intelligence, common sense, and logic may be lacking or in such abundance as to make being together not enjoyable. Perhaps one or both of you thinks too much or too little and is staying on the mental level when one of you wants things to move to the physical level. One or both of you could be moving too fast or too slow in some way, perhaps trying to move your relationship to a more intense level too quickly or not quickly enough. Or it could be that gossiping (yours or someone else's) may be causing you problems.

The solution to all of these problems is to listen. Listen to what you are saying and how you are saying it, and listen to what your partner is saying, too. Do not let your emotions cloud your ability to think logically. Be patient with yourself and others. Your relationships are in a state of flux right now. If you get annoyed because things refuse to settle down, you are only going to be more annoyed, distracted, and disappointed.

P
L
A
N
E
T
S

WORK/CAREER — *Mercury*

It is time to study and use commonsense psychology in the improvement of your work situation or in the attainment of a new and better career. It is important that you put yourself in your co-workers' shoes and see how they think of you and your job performance. It's time to learn the art of politics. It can be office politics, or getting involved with those who can help your career, or even getting involved with the politics of government in some way. Be a bridge between the people where you work and do so without creating resentment and mistrust. You might find it beneficial to work at more than one job at a time. This will bring you into contact with even more people who are in a position to help you.

Be aware of those you must connect with, though they need not be near to you physically. Connect yourself to others through books, films, instructional videos, as well as through lectures and live performances.

Learn the ways that other people have done well in the same line of work as you. With so many good things about to come into your life, it is important that you lean how other people have created their own career advancement. Making the right connections will require you to be more tolerant of others.

At this time, let your desires be known to others in a way that helps them understand how they, themselves, can benefit by helping you. The art of politics is first making the right connections and then using those connections skillfully. By doing so you will come to enjoy the kind of career you may have thought was reserved for others. Politics is the sport of the rich and powerful. It's time for you to learn how to play the game.

WEALTH/SUCCESS — *Mercury*

It is time to get busy with the details of attaining the wealth and success you desire. There is a logical pattern and methods to be learned and applied to reach your goals and now is the time to do so. Explore every opportunity that comes your way. Do not be stopped by your emotional reactions to setback, failure, or even success.

Building wealth is a game requiring discipline and the realization that small things matter. At this time, you would do better to try to accomplish many small successes, not just one or two big ones. Take things a step at a time, pay attention to every detail, and you will surely reach your goal. Neatness counts now, so make lists and plan to accomplish goals in a logical order. Try to move as quickly as you can without getting sloppy or distracted.

At this time, your best chance for attaining success would be from writing, journalism, lecturing, touring, driving, local travel, or working with your hands. There is a strong possibility that you might be able to craft a way to use your everyday routine to improve your lot in life. You could discover a way to improve an ordinary aspect of modern life in a novel way.

Investing in the communications sector would be another possibility for improving your finances. Established companies in the fields of publishing, broadcasting, the Internet, and all other methods for disseminating information would make solid choices. You would do best with smaller companies, rather than the big conglomerates, and by investing short term rather than long term.

Appreciate the fact that if you can use your mind to solve your problems, you are fortunate. Our brains are the most sophisticated computers in the world, but not everyone is fortunate enough to have theirs work correctly.

MOON

In astrology, the Moon is not only considered one of the planets, but because of its proximity to the Earth, it's importance is second only to the Sun in a person's horoscope chart. The Moon's gravitational pull produces the ebb and flow of the tides. The enchanted astrologers of old associated the Moon with our emotions, our emotional intelligence, our intuition, and the communication of all of these things which also ebb and flow. The rapid, regular passage of the Moon through the twelve signs of the zodiac is the reason it is related to our habits. Because the Moon changes shape from Full to New on a schedule so close to that of a woman's menstrual cycle, the Moon is associated with women, fertility, planting, childbirth, mothering, and nurturing in general. It also rules the relationship between a mother and her children, symbolized by the Moon watching over the Earth.

LOVE/RELATIONSHIPS — *The Moon*

At this time, your relationships are a reflection of your emotional intelligence. How you and your partner are able to feel and express your emotions will determine how well things are going for you.

If you do not have a relationship now, the reason may be related to emotional upheavals and mood swings. You could be so emotionally demonstrative and moody that you make being with you for long period of time a time extremely challenging. You could be repelled by anyone who displayed the slightest hint of being too emotional or moody. Or you could be attracted only to moody, brooding people whose emotional intelligence level makes a relationship a nightmare.

Whatever the problem you have with relationships now, it is more than likely that its origin can be found in your experience of your mother or the person who acted as your mother, if you were fortunate enough to have someone like that in your childhood. It is important that you get in touch with any emotional pain that you may have experienced, holding it up to your present difficulties with relationships and seeing where the links are. Then you must forgive your mother as the adult child she was, imagining her having you to care for and how stressful that must have been.

Forgiveness and unconditional love are the goals of every mother. Few if any are able to be that way at all times. If you find that you are unable to forgive your mother, you are in deep emotional pain and should consider professional counseling if you want your relationships to improve. You do not have to be around or even communicate with your mother if she was truly that difficult, but you do have to forgive her in your own mind. If you do not, then your relationships are always going to be sabotaged by your emotional problems.

WORK/CAREER — The Moon

You need to be empathetic now to improve your work situation. Empathy is a great help in life, especially in business. Making someone feel like you are one of their group is crucial in sales, working relationships, and job interviews. Knowing how consumers, producers, and investors are thinking can guide you to profitable business decisions. Just be careful not to let getting so close to others make you feel sorry for them.

Your intuition can also help you. Listen to your hunches. Do not be overly logical. Try blending your intuition with your logical awareness and you will see great improvement in your work and career almost immediately.

As an exercise, examine your innermost desires. If you could make as many of them real in your life as you wanted to, which of them would do the most to help you feel truly secure? You will probably find what makes you feel secure is closely related to your experiences with your family, past and present. Our needs and actions are strongly influenced by childhood security needs.

A woman, matters related to women and children, mothering, mother figures, and possibly even matters related to your own mother can affect your career in an important way now. If your relations with women and your mother are good, your career will benefit. If not, there can be trouble, so fix things right away as best as you can.

You must also be on good terms with your family to feel secure and get your career moving properly. Whoever you consider your family and how you have been getting along with them is very important to your career at this time. If things have been difficult, you must take action to make things better. Until things have been straightened out, your career will feel blocked.

WEALTH/SUCCESS — *The Moon*

A woman, possibly your mother, could improve your prosperity greatly now, either through giving you something material, an idea, or causing others to benefit you in some way. You cannot become truly wealthy unless you resolve your attitude towards women and the women in your life.

All matters related to the study of cycles and predictions, especially business cycles, are other areas that might produce material gain for you now. Things that occur monthly, on the full or new moon, or are otherwise connected with regularly occurring events can benefit you.

Your finances can improve if you use your intuition. Most successful people explain their good fortune by saying that they rely on their hunches or their "gut instinct," which is another way of saying that they have good intuition. Having a developed intuitive ability is having true wealth. Using it in harmony with our logical mind is what produces the best decisions.

At this time, moodiness can slow you down on your road to wealth and success, either your moodiness or that of someone important in your life. Being moody is a confused and embarrassed child's call for help when he wants to be seen as independent. If you are the moody one, nurture yourself more and allow family and friends to help you to feel good again. Do not punish them for not being able to wave a magic wand to make wealth and success yours. If the moodiness of another is a problem, do what you can to help, but do not get enmeshed.

If there are any children in your life, being a little over-protective is called for now. Show them that you value them more than wealth and success. If you were fortunate enough to have had a loving mother figure in your life, then appreciate her and your good fortune — even more so if she is still alive.

SUN

Though Sumerian and Babylonian astrologers knew that the Sun was a star, they counted it as a planet, the most important one. The Sun gives light and life to our world and in astrology, the Sun symbolizes our ego — us in the center of our personal solar system. The Sun is our vital life force and our identity. It is the burning desire within us to bring light and life to the world. It rules men, fatherhood, and the masculine role in life, which is to serve and protect others, especially women and children. The other planets revolve around the Sun, which is why it also rules celebrity, status, and the power to rule. If serving and protecting does not sound like it goes with being a ruler, remember that the best kind of leader is guided by what is good for all, not just for the leader's own personal gain and pleasure.

LOVE/RELATIONSHIPS — *The Sun*

If you do not have a good relationship now, the reason most likely has to do with ego — yours, the people you have met so far, or your reaction to people with too big or too little egos. You may be too concerned with status to have been able to be with people who could have been good for you. Or, your lack of ego may cause you to be ignored or even mistreated. If that is the case, try acting a little bit more like the star of your own show.

If you do have a partner, the Sun is an indication that the outlook for your love life and relationship is sunny and bright. You will have to take the lead and improve it and create the kind of relationship you want; do not expect to simply sit back and let things happen. You will have to keep things organized and moving.

You have done many wonderful things for many people in the near and distant past. Therefore, you should not feel unworthy of the most loving of relationships. Feel empowerment from the good things you have done. You cannot remember all of them, but you did them. Now see the other person in your relationship embodying your reward for being you.

You need to put yourself into the most positive situations. If you are in a place where you are happy, you will create an incredible relationship. If you are in a place where your energy has to be used just to keep things going the way they are, you could lose one of your most valuable possessions, your time. So take all possible actions to do the right thing and prepare to reap the rewards of your good deeds in the form of a great relationship.

Work/Career — *The Sun*

Even if it may not look that way today, the prospects for your work and career are excellent. Stay positive and take the high road. Act like a leader and you may find yourself being given more responsibility. Show that you know how to work for the good of all concerned and not just for your own selfish interests.

At this time, your career needs you to take a new and creative approach to solving any difficulties in which you now find yourself. The old tried and true methods will not work as well as they have in the past, unless you modify them with some new special touches. You need to be involved in projects where you are able to use and develop your creative abilities.

Creativity is fun. I am sure you would be the first to admit that you should be having more fun at what you do for a living. There are simple steps that you can use to bring the joy of creativity into even the simplest of tasks. When it comes to your career, you may not even realize how often you have already used your creativity. It is usually a question of how you refer to your creative acts before you will see how far along the road you are already. Most people call it "problem solving."

The ancient astrologers knew that our highly developed human creativity was what made us so special. Our ability to create that which had never been created before seemed to mirror the ability of Divine forces to create life itself. No matter what our circumstances, we still have the power to make an impact on our world if we choose to take the time to do so.

WEALTH/SUCCESS — *The Sun*

Success from investing and other forms of gambling is indicated now. When you take a chance, the best way to see if it is in your own best interests is to look inside yourself and see if you are enjoying yourself or are doing it out of a desperate attempt to win. Every good gambler knows the winning comes from the enjoyment derived from trying your luck. You are in a good place to experience the joy of winning now, so enjoy yourself and remember what was inscribed on the second column at the oracle at Delphi, "Nothing in excess." Savor the joy of taking a chance, do not become a slave to it. Remember to be generous with your winnings to those who have been generous to you, and to others who need and deserve your help.

At this time, you will derive much benefit from allowing your creativity free rein to create things that have never been before. All art is done mainly for the sake of doing it. The rewards given to true artists are secondary in importance to the pleasure they get just from taking the time to make their art. Exercising your creative talents, in whatever manner you enjoy, would be a wonderful way to ensure that wealth and success will flow to you.

Create things that have a "life" of their own, such as business enterprises, works of art like tapestries, plays, sculptures, novels, clothing, movies, music and many more things like that. One of the most creative things people can produce is a child, and children certainly have a life of their own. Love the children in your life as much as you can. Just being connected with children and things related to them, as well as the previously mentioned businesses and artistic enterprises, would bring you much joy and even material benefits.

SOUTH NODE

The South Node is not a planet; it is an ever-changing point of intersection between the paths the Moon and the Earth are moving in. Its symbol shows the two planets connected by a shared path, and that path is pointed south. The Hindu concept of Karma is very close to the meaning of the South Node. It symbolizes past actions we have made that we are not satisfied with. These past actions produce discomforting consequences that we must deal with to learn why we did what we did. Like astrology, itself, the South Node shows how similar, yet how different, we all are. Everyone has the South Node in his or her chart, just like everyone has done things they are not proud of. However, everyone's South

Node is in a different place relative to the position of all the other planets in their chart, symbolizing that what we must learn and how we must learn it is very different for all of us.

LOVE/RELATIONSHIPS — *South Node*

If you do not have a relationship, stop dwelling on the subject. This is not a good time for you to be looking for one. You are not in the right frame of mind to attract whom you would like to attract. You might be interested in a person who is not interested in you or not good for you. A person who you are not interested in or who is not good for you could be pursuing you. Better to seclude yourself and take appropriate action to deal with any or all of these challenges before you get back in the social scene.

You may have to deal with loss and loneliness now. No one gets through life without experiencing them. Professional help may be necessary to help you process loss. Sometimes the failure of relationship is not really anyone's fault. People grow at different rates and go in different directions. If this is the case, then be thankful for the good you had and make the break as cleanly as you can.

Rather than losing your partner, it is also possible that the mistakes you, your partner, or both of you have made are now coming back to haunt you. If so, then do not blame yourself, each other, or outsiders for your problems. Instead, look at your situation and try to see what you each may have done to cause it to manifest itself the way it has and stop that behavior immediately. Do not play the victim. What separates the successful from the unsuccessful is how they respond to problems and failure.

To get through this stressful time, take care of your health. Try not to worry if you do not see immediate improvement. Do not let your troubles affect your other relationships; you need them now more than ever.

Work/Career — *South Node*

It is time for all accounts to be settled. Stop, look, and listen. At this time, trouble regarding your work and career is indicated. It will not be easy for you to avoid having it affect you in some way. If you take all necessary and reasonable precautions to protect yourself, you will probably come through just fine.

If it was your actions or inaction that caused the trouble, change your ways now. Any bad decisions you made about your work and career could now be coming back to haunt you. Though it may be too late to keep from being fired, admit your mistakes, make amends, and demonstrate to your superiors and co-workers that you have learned from your mistakes and are ready to endure the consequences of your actions. Do not blame others or act the victim. You may have to get professional help for your trouble.

Even if you have been doing your job and staying out of trouble, there is a small chance that you could get still get fired or "downsized" or asked to retire before your time. If so, then do not waste energy blaming anyone or berating yourself for having "failed." Accept this as an opportunity to enter a new chapter of your career.

If you are out of work, you may not be able to find a paying job now, but do not stop trying. To inspire you, read some of the numerous stories about people who were fired, disgraced, poor, homeless, living on welfare, crippled, diseased, or all of these things, but who had the intestinal fortitude to endure and use their painful experiences in the creation of a new chapter of their lives and careers. This can be a productive time if you do not let your circumstances overwhelm you and cause paralysis, paranoia, and self-pity.

WEALTH/SUCCESS — *South Node*

This is not a good time for you regarding your finances, your achievements, your reputation, or any combination of these things. Stop doing what you have been doing on your quest for wealth and success, prepare for difficult times, and rethink everything. If you do not change course, the mistakes you have made will come back to haunt you. Professional help can give you true perspective on your situation.

Do not blame others for your situation. Do not play the victim. What separates the successful from the unsuccessful is how they respond to problems and failure. Successful people know they have the power to create the kind of life they want. When they suffer money problems, business losses, bad investments, or loss of their reputation, they work twice as hard to make things better and keep going, no matter what happens. This is your challenge now.

When you are trying to increase your wealth and success, there are inevitably going to be things that fail you. Other people, businesses, things like the weather, nature, the courts, and government agencies may fail you. No one can foresee and be prepared for everything. If you are not failing at something, then you are not trying everything. When people eventually succeed, their failures are referred to as life lessons.

This is a stressful time, so take care of your health. Get through it as best you can. Do not let your worries affect your interactions with those you care about. Do not deny that there are problems now regarding wealth and success. Tell them that you love them, that you are all right, and that you are working toward getting things back on track. Your troubles will pass and you will be able to get back on the road toward the wealth and success you dream of.

P
L
A
N
E
T
S

♀

VENUS

P
L
A
N
E
T
S

Venus is the planet of peace, love, beauty, and attraction, the obvious reason that its symbol is used to signify womankind. Venus rules all kinds of romantic love, marriage, romance, dating, and the basic attraction between people. It also rules pleasure of every description. Though most people think of Venus as a soft, sweet energy, it also symbolizes how desire can motivate some of the most ruthless behavior imaginable. Like Mars, the male symbol, Venus is a pure energy that must be directed properly for a person's life to run smoothly. The passion of artists is a manifestation of the properly directed power of Venus. A true artist is driven to make art no matter what the circumstances or the consequences.

All efforts to beautify or improve something, whether it is make-up for one's face, re-decorating one's home, or trying to create peace and harmony in the world are associated with our Venus energy.

LOVE/RELATIONSHIPS — *Venus*

If you do not have a relationship, you will soon attract a great one to you. Venus is the planet of romantic love and you have picked one of the best relationship cards in *The Enchanted Astrologer's* deck.

If you have a relationship that has been progressing nicely, you can expect things to get dramatically better. The love you feel is real and things may soon move to the next level, possibly a level beyond your present dreams. You may have found your soul mate.

Any problems you are now experiencing with your love life are the result of you, your partner, or both of you being blindly devoted to your vision of an ideal partner, a person who may or may not exist in reality. At some time in the near or distant past, this blind devotion set in motion forces that are affecting your present ability to give and receive love. Either you or your partner or both of you became determined to stick with this idealized vision, no matter what logic and your senses were telling you about the real person you were going with.

You can feel hurt and let down when you realize that, like you, your partner is a human being with many faults. You may feel that you still have to be, or appear to be, blindly devoted or to maintain a false personality in some other way. You may both be the victim of someone's lies.

Readjust your vision of what it is you expect from a partner. Love each other as you are and do not try to change each other into someone else. Help each other make the changes that each wants to make. You will know you are in love when you just want to be with the other person and watch him live his life naturally.

P
L
A
N
E
T
S

WORK/CAREER — *Venus*

At this time, you may expect many good things to happen to you at work and in your career. You can now attract the improvements you would like to see in your work and career, rather than working hard or going after them directly. Now is a time when being a gentle peacemaker can get you more than being aggressive. Use beauty, kindness, flattery, and make it fairly obvious what you want. Let those in a position to benefit you do so because they like and want to help you.

You may be in line for a new job that you will enjoy and where you will make a good salary. It would be best if it required you to use skills you have developed from past hard work and experiences. If your new job is too different from your past work, you may not be reminded enough of the source of your good fortune. Keep a journal and review it monthly. You will more easily see the results of your actions in this way.

This is a time when you do not have to go far to find what you are looking for, whether it is a new job or improvement with your current work situation. If you are between jobs you may find working out of your home for a time can help you gain the security you need, both financial and emotional.

You may get a raise now, but try to resist the desire to do something radical with your newfound fortune. The best thing you can do now is to solidify your position and keep supporting what has been working out well for you. Adjust to the beneficial changes brought on by the new situation and you will be in a better position to take advantage of future situations requiring big moves and long-range planning.

WEALTH/SUCCESS — *Venus*

You can attain wealth and success more easily now than at almost any other time, either on your own or through attracting other people who can help you. It is very important that you associate only with positive, success-oriented people.

It is time to take profit from what you have done. You will soon attain a major goal and you will be able to share it with a committed partner. In fact, through committed partnerships of all kinds, your good fortune is most likely going to come to you. Other people will help you even if they are not trying to do so. Now is a time when you will be able to see exactly who is on your side and who is not. This is a gift to you, if you are wise enough to use it. However, not everyone who does not agree with you should be considered an enemy.

When you wake and before you go to sleep, take five minutes to appreciate all of the good things in your life. This will attract more good things to you. To beautify your life would also produce great benefit. Buying new clothes or beautifying your appearance is the most obvious way. Beautifying your home and neighborhood, or going to a museum, a show, a dance, or any other cultural event would also be appropriate, as long as you enjoyed yourself, relaxed a little, and appreciated your life more than you had been doing.

If there are any younger people in your life, now is the time to teach them about the importance of commitment. More than just by talking, you have to teach them by your example. By doing this, you will be making the world a better place for everyone in a very real way.

P
L
A
N
E
T
S

Pluto

Pluto is the planet of power and transformation. It symbolizes the part of us that wants to get and use power of every kind. It is the planet of extremes, and so it rules our personal power to do good, but it also rules power struggles, gangsters, dictators, and the terrible things that happen when people try to make themselves powerful at the expense of others. Pluto is associated with the mysteries of life, magic, sex, and, the ultimate transformation — death. It is also associated with resurrection, whether that may be renovating a home, getting cosmetic surgery, or bringing back into your life something you thought was long gone. It represents the unconscious mind, invisible yet powerful enough to produce compulsions and obsessions seemingly beyond our control. Like Pluto, their purpose is to help us become aware of what needs to be eliminated from our life and to help us do so.

LOVE/RELATIONSHIPS — *Pluto*

If you do not have a relationship now, you may find yourself drawn to a person as if you had a spell cast over you or you may be the one who becomes the seducer. Do not do anything that goes against your better judgment to get what you think you desire or you will regret it later.

Problems in your relationships now may be the result of you, your partner (if you have one), or both of you judging each other too much or having confused sexual attractions for love. On rare occasions, drawing this card when you are asking about love and relationships is an indication that the concepts of sexual pleasure, the exchange of power, and the control of one partner by another can all be involved in your relationship.

Thinking that sex is a sin, except for procreation, leads to all kinds of problems. The desire for sexual pleasure is as natural as our other bodily functions. However, the life-altering consequences of creating a child and the life-threatening consequences of sexually transmitted diseases require that sex be treated with the utmost respect and care. Within a committed relationship, sexual passion can strengthen love and trust.

Look within and find the origin of any confusion you and your partner may have about sex and sexuality. When you find it, recreate your relationship so that the passion you now seek through the sexual intensity and excitement that others may misunderstand will last beyond the bedroom and extend into every aspect of your lives together. If you love and cherish each other for every aspect of your being, and not just as sexual playthings, you will discover many joyous aspects of life that you would otherwise never experience.

With great love comes the fear of losing it. Many people do. This is the price of love.

WORK/CAREER — *Pluto*

At this time, any trouble you are having at work is caused by the use and misuse of judgment and power, either by you, a co-worker, a superior, or a mixture of all three. There may be secrets, lies, and manipulation involved. Be careful. Do not volunteer information and keep any actions you take to protect yourself and advance your career as subtle and as secret as an international spy.

If all is well at work, then it's time for you to breathe new life into a career dream you once abandoned. At some time in the near or distant past you decided that it was impossible to pursue a career doing something that you knew you would enjoy immensely. Perhaps you were stopped by authority figures with power over you, or your own fears got in the way. You set in motion forces that required you to experience the events of the time that has passed since you abandoned this dream. If you are pursuing the career you have always wanted to, then it is time for a big change to be made. If you do not do it, circumstances or someone else will do it for you.

What was once impossible to do is now possible and you should make a serious effort to resurrect your dreams. If you are no longer aware of the dreams you once had, you may want to consult a professional counselor of some kind to assist you in getting in touch with them. The counselor you seek may even be a psychic or a practitioner of the ancient arts of astrology, tarot, and other personal oracles. You may even want to learn more about these subjects yourself.

You can resurrect your dream without abandoning your present job. When you take steps to breathe life back into your abandoned career dream, it will empower you with renewed vigor at your old job.

WEALTH/SUCCESS — *Pluto*

At this time, you may have to be a bit cold-blooded to make sure that you get what is coming to you. There may be power struggles over wealth, credit, and judgments now. Do not openly confront anyone unless you are absolutely sure that you have the resources on all levels to handle what could be used against you. Things could get quite intense. You may want to be less confrontational and work your will beneath the surface and behind the scenes. Think and act like an industrial spy. Be as secretive and subtle as you can be.

Your attitude towards wealth and specifically, towards wealthy people may be preventing you from becoming one of them. If every time you are reminded how much wealthier than you some people are, you begin an inner negative dialogue about them, you are sending yourself the message that you do not want to join their ranks. You must be of a single mind about your desire to achieve wealth and success. Your negative attitude towards wealthy people will sabotage your own efforts to become successful.

In your mind, bless them and congratulate all wealthy people you see on achieving that which you are going to achieve as well. Realize that they are just people, people who still have problems and work to do and issues are about how to keep, protect, and increase their good fortune, just like you.

Your success does not take anything away from anyone else, unless you have stolen it. There is enough wealth for all. If this was not so, how could we all get rewarded for bringing our lives into balance? We each receive according to what we ask for, and according to what we are ready to receive. It is our birthright, if we will only realize it.

P
L
A
N
E
T
S

♃

JUPITER

Jupiter, the biggest planet in our solar system, rules expansion, growth, the big picture, thinking big, being jovial, generous, and fortunate. Jupiter symbolizes our capacity to grow as human beings — in our work, in our relationships, and every other area of our life. Jupiter rules plain luck, but also the true fortune that is the result of expanding one's mind through learning and being open to new ideas. This enables a person to see and take advantage of opportunities another person might overlook. Jupiter rules expansion of all kinds, whether buying another business adding a room, or increasing the size of our waistline. It rules abundance and it also rules too much of a good thing. When Jupiter energies are operating in your life, things will not go badly even if you just do nothing. However, when you work hard during one of those times, the results can be spectacular good luck.

LOVE/RELATIONSHIPS — *Jupiter*

If you do not have a relationship, get ready to get lucky and have one of the biggest and most positive experiences of your lifetime. Your new partner could be larger than life in some way. She or he could even be a teacher or even a wealthy or foreign person. You will definitely be with someone you enjoy being with immensely.

If you are in a relationship, you can expect things to work well and improve greatly. You will feel blessed by good fortune on many levels.

Any problems you are now experiencing are probably caused by outside influences interfering with your efforts to improve relationship. Friends, family, or others, may have influenced you so greatly that you are accepting what they have told you even when it goes against what you know to be true. You may or may not have realized how far their influence has reached. It is time to get in touch with what you believe to be true, not what you have been told is true. To create a loving relationship you must know who you are, what you believe in and what it is that you want and need.

Be careful not to live your life based on the opinions or the gossip of others. Keep in mind this influence may be coming from newspapers, magazines, books, TV, radio and all other outside sources and not just through people you actually know. You may be unduly influenced by fashion and other fads.

Once you know that you are living your life true to your own beliefs, you will be amazed at how a passion for what really matters to you will return. You may start traveling more, drawn to the romance of foreign people, places, and things because they represent a complete and unique way of looking at the world.

PLANETS

WORK/CAREER — *Jupiter*

At this time, there is tremendous potential for new and exciting developments in your work and career. However, to bring these good times into your life requires you to broaden your perspective about your work. It is no longer sufficient for you to think small. It is time to think big, as if you owned the company you work for. You may even be able to start your own business, even if you keep your present job.

You are at a wonderful time in your life when the possibilities for an exciting career are all around you. It could even be called a "lucky" time. A good definition of a lucky time, in terms of work and career, is when your preparations meet a golden opportunity. So be prepared for the golden opportunities that will soon be coming your way.

If you are out of work, you can expect to get at least one great job offered to you, though you will probably get more than one. It may require you to travel or become involved in the travel business, higher education, publishing, the law, philosophy, or broadcasting.

This is a great time to read books written by or about people who have succeeded in doing what you would like to do. Find out how people in foreign countries have approached your line of work. Blending their ideas with yours may be the way to go.

Now is the time to enjoy your good fortune and expand your beliefs about what is possible for you to accomplish with your life. Just thinking about that subject will open your eyes to all kinds of possibilities. When the time comes to get down to the hard work of making your dreams come true, it will not seem like hard work at all.

WEALTH/SUCCESS — *Jupiter*

This is a lucky time for you and you can expect your wealth and success to increase considerably. It is a time to spend money and make money. There will be expansion in all areas of your life so watch that your newfound good fortune does not show too much on your waistline. It is a time to increase your awareness of what is going on in the world and the many opportunities available to you. Spend money on travel that helps you expand your understanding of the world. People from foreign countries could be of great help to you now.

It would be a great time to move to a bigger place or expand the size of your present living or working space. You can expect to find many opportunities to improve all aspects of your life.

Publishing, education, and broadcasting can benefit you. Investing in big or foreign companies is also favored. Anything to do with reading, writing, teaching, and learning are all favored. The information coming to you from those sources will also give you a new sense of what is possible in your life. Contests and games of chance may be easier to win now than at almost any other time.

Your judgment is very good now and you may be called upon to help others decide what is the right thing to do. More than any other time, honesty is the best policy for you now, so don't hold back on the truth. The power of positive thinking will seem to work like magic for you. Be positive at all times. You will soon realize that happiness comes by living it in all your moods and actions. Try singing and chanting more to reinforce how happy and thankful you are to be alive and as lucky as you are.

P
L
A
N
E
T
S

♄ SATURN

Saturn is the planet of structure, time, boundaries, restriction, and discipline. It helps you delay pleasure so that you can do what needs to be done in the time allotted for it. Saturn is a stern teacher, but it can reward you for enduring your burdens in a mature manner. Conversely, if you shirk your responsibility, Saturn will show you the error of your ways. It represents adulthood, authority and the long period of hard work and determination necessary to become an authority. The respect that people have for those in authority is also the province of Saturn, as is fame, a close cousin of respect. Saturn is the last planet usually visible to the naked eye and so it is associated with going as far as you can go in life, especially in your career. Its love for giving structure to systems and making them function at peak efficiency makes Saturn the most business-like planet. It also rules automobiles, antiques, and crystals.

LOVE/RELATIONSHIPS — *Saturn*

If you do not have a relationship, the reason is probably related to how you feel about structure, limits, and discipline. You may be so disciplined that you do not leave any room in your life for a relationship, possibly because you think it will distract you from more serious, important matters. Or you could be so undisciplined that you scare away prospective partners. It could also be that you do not want to get involved with anyone who displays either too much or too little self-discipline. You may be too limited in your thinking and unwilling to give people a chance to be human. You may be thought a wet blanket.

You may want a partner who is older, a teacher, or who provides a stern hand. You might want to be that person for anyone you get intimate with. Or you may fear anyone who might try to impose any kind of discipline, limits, or structure to your life. This would limit the number of people you could have a relationship with, but it is a part of the structure of your being and must be honored.

In all of your relationships, now is the time to get serious. The level of commitment must be stated clearly before there is any action taken to live together. Living together is the same thing as marriage for some, while for others it is an arrangement of convenience. At this time, you could not have a casual relationship.

If your present committed relationship has gotten too serious and limiting, it is very important that the two of you begin a slow, patient, and loving dialogue about how things have gotten to the state they are in. Then you can make a fun, sexy, but structured plan to lighten things up.

WORK/CAREER — *Saturn*

Recognition and reward for your hard work will soon be here. Your good example will be used to urge others on to their own achievements. Be conservative in the truest sense of the word now. Get involved in the conservation of resources of all kinds. This includes time, money, possessions, and both natural resources and those that are the result of manufacturing and technological processes.

If you are between jobs, you will soon be offered one. It may not be glamorous, but it will be a great opportunity. Every person and every business goes through lean times. It is only the best people who can get a business through the hard times. By dressing and acting conservatively, you will give a feeling of comfort to those above you. They need to be able to depend on you now. Show them that you know how to be punctual, persistent, and that you know how to structure your job and any business systems you are responsible for in the most efficient and productive manner. They may ask you to help reorganize other departments.

If you see mistakes being made by those in a position to help advance your career, act in the most cautious manner you are capable of. Do not do anything that will bring blame to them; that would delay your reward. Do what you can to make things work smoothly, even if you have to fix things in such a way that no one realizes it is you who is making things work. Your reward will be much more enjoyable than mere praise, so take a deep breath, hold your tongue and do your job better than you have ever done it before. The increase in power, wealth, and prestige that is coming your way will more than compensate you for any minor inconveniences.

Wealth/Success — *Saturn*

You may become recognized as an authority or rewarded for your hard work. It is even possible that your reputation may soon extend beyond your usual circles.

This is a good time to seek the advice and wise council of people you respect and authority figures in general. They will help you, both materially and to understand the adjustments that will be required of you to live with more wealth and success. With increased status will come not only increased rewards but also increased responsibilities. If you find your responsibilities increasing, take that as a sign of your approaching financial success.

You will take well to this new increase in responsibilities. In fact, another sign of your success will be an increase in your respect for those who know how to be patient and self-disciplined. You will follow their good example and will set an example for others to follow.

You can expect material comforts and benefits to come from people in power positions and other authority figures. You will naturally be able to work well with those who used to be your superiors in some way. Now, they can see you as a person who deserves respect and will be treating you accordingly.

Take time every day to appreciate your capacity for endurance and perseverance. When the good times come, you will be rewarded for all of the parties and good times you missed. It is crucial that you appreciate yourself and your accomplishments in a way that you never have before. In fact, give yourself an award, a reward, something you have been putting off until you were a success. Feel that you are a success now. You do not have to wait any longer to allow yourself to feel that you are successful. You have made it.

P
L
A
N
E
T
S

Uranus

Uranus is the planet of eccentricity, genius, rebelliousness, revolution, and invention. It is the forces in our life that want to keep things new, exciting, and on the edge. There is a nervous quality to Uranus that is the result of its unpredictable nature. The planet Uranus is the only planet that points its North Pole at the Sun as it circles it once every eighty years. It symbolizes the crisis of middle age that occurs at age forty, when we are tested to see if we have made our life a statement of our unique individuality. If we have, we are rewarded. If not, then all kinds of out-of-the-blue things happen to goad us out of our rut. Uranus rules electricity and electrical devices like computers, radios and television sets, dynamite and all explosives, and especially futuristic devices. Uranus is the planet of crazy theories and science fiction that will one day be revealed as scientific fact.

LOVE/RELATIONSHIPS — *Uranus*

If you do not have a partner, feel free to try something new. Go to completely different kinds of places to meet people, even places you might have thought were too bizarre before. Be open to new and different types of people, the exact opposites of the kinds you may have been associating with in the past.

It is important to keep any relationship new and exciting. If you have done that, then your relationship is stronger than ever and ready for any unexpected challenges that might arise. If you have allowed things to get stuck at the same old level with no growth or change to speak of, then get to work fixing it now or your relationship will soon be tested by one or both of you acting rebelliously or disruptively, out-of-the blue challenges, or both.

The planet Uranus challenges you with unexpected events that cause you, eventually, to feel liberated, refreshed, and more alive than ever. These events disrupt the status quo in your life and the lives of those around you. However, if you bring newness into your life on your own terms, Uranus will not have to. All relationships can change for the better. That is what makes them so attractive in the first place.

Both people in any relationship must feel free and independent. This may sound like a contradiction in terms, but people in a successful relationship can tell you that they have actually found the freedom to be themselves fully through their relationship. Be true to yourself and your spirit of independence. If you can do that, you will improve an existing relationship. If you don't have one, you will attract to you someone who is drawn by the real you. Nothing is more enjoyable than to be appreciated for who you really are.

P
L
A
N
E
T
S

Work/Career — *Uranus*

Matters related to your work and career are not going to be very stable for a time. There could be revolution brewing and you have to decide which side you are on. If negative business trends, unfair or oppressive conditions, or outmoded ways of thinking have been going on for so long that they have become intolerable, there may be a sudden release of energies that could be quite disruptive.

Even if things are proceeding smoothly at work, it is time for some new approaches. You may be called upon to be the agent of this change or you may be a bit too set in your ways. If you are wondering why things have not been working out for you lately, the answer may lie in your attitude toward the changes that must now occur to keep things new, exciting, interesting, and moving toward your goal. Now is the time in your career where resisting change and just grinning and bearing the present situation will probably do more harm than good.

If you are between jobs or career matters have been truly disappointing of late, then it is time to make changes in your line of work. Changing jobs, a new job description, a change of style or location are all things to consider. Allow yourself to explore those areas of life that you have been putting off until tomorrow. Jobs with a future, jobs that are actually involved with futuristic technologies like electronics, biotech, telecom, the Internet, and space exploration would all be good for you now.

Start from right where you are with a decision that you will be open to new possibilities for career growth and changes. Feel with all your heart that change is possible. Realize that you cannot attain your goals without big changes occurring in your life.

WEALTH/SUCCESS — *Uranus*

This is an unstable time. It can be a time for your hopes and wishes to materialize in a startling unusual way, or you could suffer a sudden reversal of fortune. The only thing you can expect is the unexpected. If you have often thought that your life had settled down into an all too predictable routine and wished for more excitement in your life, you are about to get your wish.

Inventions of all kinds are favored now. Wealth and success can come to you as a result of you or someone else coming up with a new or different way of creating wealth. If you come up with an idea that you think can be sold during this time, pursue it. Patent attorneys and venture capitalists would be receptive, especially to ideas for making people's lives better and longer and businesses more productive. Be careful to work only with reputable people.

Computers and electronics are also favored now. A futuristic technology could be easy for you to understand and profit from now. You could see how it could be genuinely useful. You would understand the basic trends that would be materializing in the future in any area you are familiar with. You would be able to accurately predict how things would turn out for you and your friends.

The wealth and success that you have dreamed of may be about to begin manifesting themselves in your life. Expect them to arrive in unusual, exciting, and even somewhat disturbing ways. This is especially likely if you have been working hard to escape lack of wealth and success. Although the events may disturb your routine, you will look back on them with marvel at the way they were able to bring newness into your life in ways that nothing else could have done so.

NEPTUNE

Neptune is the planet of transcendent beauty and inspiration, like that of nature. It rules theories about dimensions beyond this one, faith, and the belief in things that we cannot see, the power of prayer, and the afterlife. Neptune rules the thoughts and the things that give us goose bumps because they are so noble and great. It is the ideal of everything that we are all trying to achieve, so perfect that it may not exist in this world. Neptune also rules films and gases and everything else that clouds our worldly vision and forces us to use all of our senses, including our intuition. When the beauty and idealization of Neptune become clouded by fear or personal desires, the tendency to want to escape can be as overwhelming as the ocean's currents. This is why Neptune is also associated with drugs, alcohol, and other escapist behavior. It also rules psychic phenomena, when we may actually visit the realms of spiritual power beyond our earthly one.

LOVE/RELATIONSHIPS — *Neptune*

If you do not have a relationship now, the problem may be caused by trying to escape from reality in some way. Any dependence on drinking, drugs, cults, or even traditional religion will prevent you from being yourself and seeing people for who they really are. You do not want to get involved in a relationship where to get or keep your partner you have to deceive her or him, yourself, or others, or give up your beliefs and identity.

This is an unclear time and you are feeling vulnerable. If you are not treated extremely well by your partner, your relationship may very well dissolve, especially if you have given too much of yourself and asked too little of your partner in return. You may not have asked your partner to give you what you are entitled to have. You may have lived both for the other person and through the other person; this has diluted your sense of self-worth and is affecting your love life today.

If you thought that love required giving of yourself selflessly and without expecting anything in return, then quite naturally you feel unsatisfied by this kind of relationship. This is not true love. In your heart, you knew then what you know now: the loving relationship you seek is one where you and your partner give and receive from each other in equal measure.

You deserve to have your support from your partner. When that happens, you will either improve your current relationship greatly or find a new one that will bring you much peace and joy. Until you do, you may continue to experience problems that are preventing you from enjoying the relationship you are destined to have. You must respect yourself and your needs or no one else will do so, either.

P
L
A
N
E
T
S

WORK/CAREER — *Neptune*

At this time, how comfortable you are with your emotions and your attitude toward intuitive knowledge hold the key to bringing you the kind of job you have always wanted. At some time in the near or distant past, you set in motion forces that required you to suppress or ignore your emotions and intuitive hunches about things. Perhaps you did not want emotional concerns to prevent you from doing your job or being promoted. Perhaps you did not want to risk being labeled as odd in a negative way. Now your career requires you to balance your efforts to make money with a real concern for the emotional well being of all concerned.

In fact, you will do better still if you listen to your intuition and use it carefully to guide your logical decisions. The most successful people in the world are those who have learned the great benefits to be derived from harnessing their intuitive and logical abilities together to achieve their goal. This is a great power and using it will bring you the kind of career that you have always dreamed of having. Many of the world's great discoveries were realized in dreams and daydreams.

If you find it hard to understand how your emotional and intuitive development and that of others could be affecting your career, this shows you have the greatest need to re-connect with those aspects of your life. Even if you have been ignoring your feelings and intuitions, or the feelings of others, your emotional life has continued to play an important, though unacknowledged, role in your life. Without the benefit of your logical mind to guide it, however, you will not be able to reap the rewards you deserve.

WEALTH/SUCCESS — *Neptune*

This is not a time for ego gratification. It is a time to help others in a truly charitable spirit. Act as an agent for bringing assistance to others. Besides the personal actions that you know you need to take to help those you care about, you would gain a wealth of spirit by taking part in the kind of charitable acts that are done through relief agencies, religious agencies, hospitals, prisons, and even the charitable divisions of large institutions. This is a time to be aware of those less fortunate than you and to help them in whatever small way you can.

You may experience good fortune and possibly even material gain now, but it is most likely that you will experience this as answers to your prayers for assistance. For this reason, it is very important that you should be precise about what you want and should pray on a regular basis.

If you bring charity and service work into the mix with your for-profit work, you can expect to experience remarkable events in your life. Those you have wronged will forgive you now and you can forgive others, a great way of clearing your spirit and re-establishing your feeling of connection with the world. Now is a time when great benefit can come to you from realizing the many ways we are all connected.

Give thanks for what you have and be proud of what you have made of your life. Reverse the incorrect notion that people can only be spiritual if they suffer poverty or lack. Your success can show many others how good life can be when you know what you want, pray for it, and are willing to do all you can to help others as unseen forces help you make your prayers come true.

I

1st House

The First House is all about you — your appearance, how you think about yourself, and how you choose to project yourself in relationships with other people. You are the star of your own show. Your personality, appearance, and attitude about yourself determine how you will experience your life. Your First House is also known as your "Rising Sign" and your "Ascendant." It is determined by the exact time of your birth because it is the degree out of the 360 degrees of the zodiac that was exactly on the horizon as you took your first breath. If you were born at sunrise, you are a true representation of your astrological sign. If your Rising Sign is very different than your Sun Sign, your true nature and your intentions will not be apparent to other people, especially to those who do not know you very well or are unwilling to see you for who you really are.

LOVE/RELATIONSHIPS — 1st

If you do not have a relationship, the reason may be that you fear that having one means giving up your individuality and personal freedom. Or you may like your life the way it is, though other people might not understand that. You may also feel, rightly or wrongly, that you have a lot of work to do on yourself before you can get involved with someone else's life.

Even if you have a relationship, you may have to overcome some very conflicted feelings about whether or not you have the right to look out for your own interests. You do have this right. However, some people consider this a very egotistical or even an aggressive way to live. The best relationship for you now is one where you can be yourself without restriction. You must be able to speak your mind forcefully, even if it is something that your partner or a perspective partner does not want to hear.

Avoid being held back by other people's wants, needs, and habits. Do not give up on yourself or your dreams. Associate only with those who support you and your dreams of the future. Allow all those you encounter to respond to the real you. To be surrounded by interesting, self-assured, and admiring friends, you must first become secure enough to know what you like and dislike about people, places, and things.

Remember that having good self-esteem does not mean thinking and acting like you have no faults. It is possible and very beneficial for you to be aware of your faults, especially if you can do so without thinking that you are a bad person for having any faults in the first place. We all have faults; being aware of them is the first step to learning how to cope with them.

Work/Career — 1st

It is time to examine closely your attitude about work. Do your job as if you owned your company. If you cannot work for or by yourself now, it is important that you be able to work without too much interference. It is time to formulate a plan for the advancement of your career while you are immersed in the reality of your work. You cannot distract yourself now with the needs and goals of other people.

In the recent or distant past, you demonstrated to yourself that you have the ability to work well with others. You helped others to shine and were content to share the glory with the group. Now, it is time for you to lead. You have something unique to contribute to any team and if they do not let you do so, you must take your contribution elsewhere. Your innovative ideas are a rare commodity that must be valued and acted on immediately. It is time for you to show you have the rare ability to be able to work on your own or with minimal supervision.

If you cannot get over feeling impatient with the pace of others or with the speed of your career's advancement, then why try to deny it? However, avoid being too honest about that. Your challenge is no longer to prove that you can work with others and like it. You see, you are in a situation where it is not as important whether or not others may think you are competing with them. Like it or not, you are competing with them. It is good to test the accuracy of your beliefs by stating them forcefully and seeing if others can challenge them. Just keep in mind that not everyone has the time or the strength to play this game with you too often.

WEALTH/SUCCESS — 1st

Wealth and success can come to you now from ideas that are related to you personally. You may get an idea because of an experience or a need that you have, and translate it creatively into something that can benefit you and others.

Wealth and success can come to you now but only as a result of your own efforts. It is not going to be given to you. You are on your own now, but that is a good thing. Focus on your desires for the time being. Start from where you are now and use all the resources you already have available to you, but expect no one to give you much help now.

You will succeed in proportion to the amount of time and energy you have been putting out to do your best and not to be the best. Doing your best energizes you and everyone whom you meet. Trying to be the best puts too much emphasis on forces beyond your control.

If there are young people in your life, accept them as the unique individuals they are. In return, they will make you feel better about how well you have done for yourself and for them. You can no longer make them fit into anyone else's plan as to what they should be doing with their lives. It is time for you to be a shining example to them of what it means to be your own person.

Though it may feel odd at first, make a regular time each day to love yourself more and appreciate your good traits and accomplishments. Most of us are too hard on ourselves because of the misguided notion that this will spur us on to be better and work harder. Loving yourself is essential to having the wealth and success you desire.

H
O
U
S
E
S

2

2ND HOUSE

The Second House is related to your resources – everything that is available to help you live your life the way you want. Like all of the houses, its meaning can be interpreted on the material, the mental, and the spiritual level. This is why the Second House is about money and material possessions, but it is also about your mental attitude about your resources, and your ultimate value system. What you consider valuable and precious will determine what you go after and what you keep out of your life. Many people trying to walk a spiritual path think they have to avoid money and material possessions. However, it is greed – the love of money and the seduction of the material world – and the belief that what we own determines our value that must be avoided. A resource that is often squandered is time, another area of life "ruled" by the Second House.

LOVE/RELATIONSHIPS — *2nd*

Relationships now depend on how much your actions are true to your value system. If you are staying true to what you believe, things are going to improve greatly and you will be fulfilled. If you are going against what you know to be right, things are not going to go well.

If you do not have a relationship now, it may be because of your present attitude and past experiences regarding money, possessions, and the resources available to you to live the way you want to live. Partnered or not, the way you (or another person) conducted yourself with regard to money and possessions in the past is now affecting your love life. If you have co-mingled your resources with that of a partner, and things are not going smoothly, you may have to separate out what is yours to put things back on an even footing.

Seek a relationship where you value each other because of who you are, not because of what you have. All too often, people tend to judge each other and make assumptions about each other based on how much wealth they possess. Many wonderful relationships have never come to pass because some people look at potential love interests as if they were potential financial backers.

A relationship lasts when it is a union of two independent people who are secure in as many ways as possible. Being with people because of what they can offer you and not for who they are will not lead to happiness. Money and possessions are resources available to you to fulfill your life's purpose. Try thinking of money and possessions as if they were the kind of true love that you want to give and receive and watch more of both of them come to you.

WORK/CAREER — *2nd*

It is time to go where the money is. If you are not being paid what you are worth, you must either get a raise or investigate other places, or even other lines of work, that can pay you what you are worth.

Troubles at work require you to see if you or someone else is being greedy, or if too much importance is being put on a situation that does not deserve it. It would be equally valuable for you to discover whether or not a potentially profitable situation is being wasted for lack of the proper attention. New business is all well and good, but leave that to others until you are sure that existing job situations have been dealt with properly.

A career where your taste for the finer things in life would benefit you may come into the picture now. If you are younger, it could benefit you to take what is an entry-level position in a career connected with providing luxuries for the well-to-do. If you are older, consulting work would work for you.

Another manifestation of the attention to values in your career is to actually work in the financial realm of the business world. Existing financial resources must be properly allocated, used, and developed. Conserve and be conservative. Make a note of all obstacles you believe to stand in the way of what you know you should have, but do not feel that you have to bring any major actions to a head at this time. March steadily on doing what you are doing and gather strength from your accomplishments. Later on, you will be glad that you took this time to assess your situation and consolidate the benefits of past efforts. Doing so will expose you to opportunities that you would otherwise have never imagined were so close to home.

Wealth/Success — *2nd*

It is a very lucky time for you now. Money and other material rewards can come to you easily and in many forms simultaneously. You will soon have more of the kinds of comfort and luxuries you have wanted. A long period of waiting is over.

Like the slow, steady turning of the Earth, your persistent efforts to attain wealth and success have been unstoppable. You are about to be rewarded in measure to how true to your value system you have been. You will soon cease worrying so much about money. Even if it seems like things are going the same old way, expect a great stroke of luck to arrive, the result of much planning and endurance on your part. You have thought of many ways to create money. Your patience will pay off in ways you never even dreamed of.

Be practical and you'll ensure that you will have enough when you need it the most. What resources you have saved for the future will stand you in good stead. This does not always have to be money or wealth in the material sense. What you consider necessary for your own success is what is important. The strength of your faith is as important as any material resource.

A period of stability is coming, a time when you can catch your breath and see where your life has taken you. You will be able to take the time to spend with friends and family, your true wealth.

Appreciate whatever resources you have now as the blessings and rewards they are. Be thankful that you are on the fast track to wealth and success now. Making a time each day to give thanks for what you have can make you even luckier than you are.

3RD HOUSE

The Third House is the house of relating and relations. It is connected with communications of all kinds, both the kind you make in person and through the use of speech, writing, sign language, body language, facial expressions, code, and other methods, too. It also rules the means for such communications, such as writing implements, books, telephones, computers, wireless devices, pagers, televisions, satellites, wire, radios, and everything you can imagine. It also rules puzzles, gossip, and mental work. Communicating often requires that you move yourself to a different location, and so the Third House rules travel done with a practical purpose in mind, especially going to school to master the basics of a subject before you are able to use it in your own way. It is the house of busy-ness, taking care of the routine things that are the necessities of life. We have used a butterfly to symbolize this house, to symbolize short distance travel, and to remind us that the ordinary and routine are incredibly beautiful.

LOVE/RELATIONSHIPS — *3rd*

If you are not in a relationship, you might find one through your siblings or even through your other relatives. You would be likely to meet someone interesting while taking classes or on-the-job training. A relationship might come to you in a place where you go or have been many times, a place you would ordinarily take for granted, like where you work, go to school, go shopping or even on your way to or from a place like that.

If you are in a relationship, any problems you are experiencing may be the result of the inability of either one of you to relate to the other. There may be too much of a difference between you in one or more areas; upbringing, schooling, religion, type of work, friends, work ethics, basic philosophy, and a host of other differences may have driven a wedge between you. One or both of you may be feeling completely misunderstood.

You must communicate clearly that you want your relationship to survive and prosper, if you do. Then you must make an effort to relate to each other and understand your differences. You may be so busy that there is the danger that a romantic relationship can manifest too much "brother and sister" energy and not enough romance. If that is so, communicate your affection, show your desire, and make time for romantic interludes, no matter what.

Avoid gossip if you do not want to spend your time dealing with hurt feelings. Choose your words carefully and make sure you are understood. Two people can hear the same words but interpret them in radically different ways.

It is important that you keep a journal about your relationships. Seeing your thoughts on paper would help you clarify many areas of your life, not just love and relationships. The written word has power and it is time for you to see the power of your thoughts put down on paper.

WORK/CAREER — *3rd*

It is important that you are on time to all appointments or you might miss connecting with a great job opportunity. Check all of your travel plans thoroughly and allow yourself plenty of time to meet those with whom you have appointments. Let them be the ones who are late, not you. Even traveling to and from those appointments might be beneficial in some way.

It is time for you use your existing connections to advance yourself. Sometimes, it is not what you know but whom you know. Any discomfort you feel with this all too obvious fact of life reveals the amount of work you will have to do before you are able to advance yourself.

Benefit may come through your siblings, relatives, neighbors, and co-workers so make sure you are on good terms with all of them. You can find common ground with people who are in a position to benefit you. It is unreasonable to expect people to help your career until they know you and your abilities. Get to know them and they will help you in their own ways.

Anyone who does not understand your motives regarding your network of contacts is someone you should either educate or avoid altogether. Do not waste your time on those people who are not willing to expand their understanding of how things work.

Making the right connections will teach you many things about people you may have thought you did not like. In this way, you will get close to the universal ideal of loving all.

If you do not have a job, take the first one that comes. Occupations that you would do well at now are communications, publicity, journalism, accounting, computers, and all skills requiring you to meet a lot of new people on a regular basis.

WEALTH/SUCCESS — 3rd

This would be a good time to learn all you can about accumulating and managing money. Reading books and taking courses would be very beneficial. You might also ask a successful sister, brother, or relative to give you advice about how to attain your goals. Whatever you learn must become a part of your everyday routine.

Investments related to communications, publishing, transportation, schools, and education can benefit you now. Whatever you invest in, you should get out and see for yourself what they do. If you cannot visit every place, your old school friends can help you in this and other ways.

If there are children in your life, do not expect to be seeing as much of them as you would like. At this time, you may find that both you and these children become more dependent upon relatives and neighbors to help you keep your life functioning at home. For this reason, it is especially important that you know the basic important information about any people on whom you are depending. You would be surprised at how many people, especially those who are as busy as you, do not take the small amount of time to know exactly who it is they are putting so much responsibility on. Getting involved with picking a nanny or a school may seem like an extra burden, but it will pay off.

This is a time when you could be receiving recognition, gifts, prizes, and awards from activities involving you with relatives, neighbors, schools, and communities. A quiz, puzzles, riddles, or contests related to famous quotes or products and services you use everyday will be the ones most likely to bring you rewards. Appreciate the wealth of your eyesight, manual dexterity, and your ability to communicate, if you are fortunate enough to have these gifts. Do not take anything for granted.

HOUSES

4TH HOUSE

The Fourth House is all about what home, family, and the past mean to you. It is where you are coming from, both literally and figuratively. It represents your inner-self, who you are when you are home and no one is watching or listening. It is about what makes you feel secure. It usually is related to how you experienced your mother or the parent or parental figure that cared for and nurtured you the most and gave you any unconditional love, if you were lucky enough to receive any while you were growing up. Now that you are older, the Fourth House is related to your past — including your past experiences, people, and places from your past, and how you feel about them. It is also related to buying, selling, renting, and owning land, buildings, apartments, condos and other fixed forms of wealth.

Love/Relationships — *4th*

It is important that any relationship you are in now makes you feel secure. When you are with your partner, you should feel at home and like you have no need to be anywhere else. A relationship from your past may come back into your life now. If you do not have a relationship now, you may soon become attracted to someone who reminds you of someone you used to know and care about. You may be surprised at how your maternal feelings rise within you now.

Any problems you are now experiencing with your love life are probably the result of things you experienced as a child. This could range from simply you and your partner coming from very different upbringings to serious traumas one or both of you suffered as children, the wounds of which are still felt.

If you are not in a relationship, spend this time making your home into the kind of secure nest where a great relationship can be born. Now is not the time for going out every night. Love may just knock on your door. Also possible is that a relationship may come to you now through family or people you consider your family.

In modern psychology much emphasis has been placed on the importance of getting in touch with experiences of our childhood. However, there has not been equal emphasis placed on the value of constructive living — of taking responsibility for who you are now, and letting your involvement with the issues at hand put the past in its proper place. Even if your own childhood was extremely happy or sad, trying to apply experiences from your past to the present situation without enough consideration for the present conditions can create a great deal of stress for you and your partners. Learn from the past, but live in the moment.

H
O
U
S
E
S

WORK/CAREER — *4th*

Examine what you believe it would take to make you feel secure in your work and career. Then formulate a plan to bring that security into your life.

At some time in the near or distant past your efforts to gain career advancement were made from a position of desperation. You did not allow yourself what you thought was the luxury of addressing your own needs. Now that way of thinking and acting is no longer appropriate. In fact, if you do not take the time to stop and think about what it is that would really make you feel secure, you will put a roadblock in the way of your new career success. You cannot get what you want until you know what you want, so you must become aware of what it is that will make you feel secure. Once you are clear about that, security like you have never known can be yours and more quickly than you would ever think possible.

It is important that you do not take any unnecessary risks for a while. There are opportunities for career advancement all around you, but you must feel safe and protected to make the best use of them. You do not have to go far from your home and family to find what it is you have longed for. Working at home would enable you to spend more time with your family, which is exactly what you should do at this time. Not only would you be able to devote more attention to your support system, but also you would best be able to examine your feelings about your home and family. Your relationship with your family holds the key to when you will finally be achieving the kind of new and exciting career you have been waiting for.

Wealth/Success — *4th*

This is a good time to profit from the work and advice of your close family, people from your past, and from long-term investments of many kinds. If you have made any in the past, then they would be coming to fruition and now would be a good time to take your profits. If not, then now would be a good time to make such an investment. Retirement planning is especially favored now. Real estate, especially real estate you or your family intend to live on, is also a good bet. Any and all improvements that you make to where you live will be very good investments, too. Whether you live in a cave or a castle, making it more comfortable, more beautiful, and safer would be money well spent now. Collecting original art or crafts would feed your soul, something that is very necessary to achieve true wealth and success.

Awards and recognition are most likely to come from organizations connected with your home or your past, or if they are concerned with families, products for the home, or family values. If you want to enter any lotteries, you would do better to enter with close friends and family. Using numbers important to family members would be more likely to work for you than at other times.

If you were having financial problems, now would be a good time to turn to your close family or people who you have chosen to be your new family for help. They would be more inclined to help now then at other times. If you do not obtain help from those close to you, expect to have to pledge your home or something that is equally vital to your security to secure your loan.

H
O
U
S
E
S

5

5TH HOUSE

The Fifth House is related to your ability to be creative, to be lucky, and to enjoy life. The ability to approach life's challenges creatively exists in everyone, but not everyone is willing to take a chance on himself. Though it is a lot of fun, creating something that has never existed before requires hard work, giving up control, and exposing yourself to criticism, misunderstanding, and ridicule. That is why the Fifth House is also related to making art of all kinds — children, romance, acting, design, music, architecture and creative endeavors of all kinds. They all take on a life of their own that is beyond one's control. Gambling, investments, sports, and risk-taking in every way are also Fifth House matters. The purpose of life is to be happy and the Fifth House is the house of what makes us happy. It is the thrill of life as the ultimate amusement park ride and the scariest of movies all rolled into one.

LOVE/RELATIONSHIPS — 5th

The time for fun, games, and — above all — romance is now. No matter how busy you are, you have to make time in your schedule for romantic interludes. A relationship that allows you to experience the romantic thrill of first meeting will become strengthened and very rewarding. A relationship where there is no romance is in danger of ending.

If you do not have a relationship, you soon will. The Fifth House is the house of romance, so have fun and you will find love. Sometimes you have to take a chance on the fact that it is possible to find love and this is one of those times.

Relationships with children will also be very good now. If you do share in the raising of children they will be a source of pride and joy to you both.

Problems in existing relationships may be the result of not making time for fun and romance, or poor results from investments and calculated risks. There is also the possibility that children may be the problem, or your views on children may conflict, especially about the conditions that have to be present before children can be brought into the world and reared properly.

Children are neither a solution nor a problem regarding your relationship. These are two separate issues. When you can admit that they are a great joy, a separate kind of problem, and a great responsibility that cannot be ignored, you will be on your path to a healthy relationship with someone. Having children without consideration of its effect on your life will create an almost overwhelming amount of work for you. Bringing children into this world without being able to provide for them physically, emotionally, intellectually, and spiritually will make having an ideal relationship an extremely challenging endeavor.

H
O
U
S
E
S

WORK/CAREER — 5th

It is very important that you do work that allows you to some-how express your ability to create solutions to problems and make general improvements. A career opportunity in the arts should be pursued. If you have ever thought of acting, now is the time to try auditioning for a part. Other jobs that may manifest themselves are investing, sports related work, gaming of all kinds, and opportunities to display goods, either for advertisements or in the places where they are sold. You may also find yourself called on to do some public speaking, another opportunity to display your creativity "on stage".

One of the most important things to keep in mind when you are taking the first steps to actualize your creativity is your warming up period. Although most people think that fear of the criticism of others is what is preventing them from doing what they really want to do, this is not often the case. Usually, it is our own self-criticism that is much more than enough to stop us dead in our tracks. Being aware that you must go through a warming up period will get you over the wall of your own self-criticism as well as when your creative efforts are seen by other people, too.

Do not expect your first efforts to be the masterpiece of creativity you will be making in the future. It is enough that you just apply yourself to your work and do what you can, knowing that you are warming up, getting the feel of your creative powers. Keep yourself from judging your first creative efforts and put all your effort into your work. Leave criticism to the critics. We all know that many critics are actually frustrated practitioners of what they love to criticize.

WEALTH/SUCCESS — 5th

This is one of the luckiest cards you can draw. Your good fortune can best come to you through having fun, enjoying love and romance, and being creative. In whatever you do, if you can look at it as fun, things will work out fabulously in your favor. If you can look at even your routine tasks as pleasurable, you will bring wealth and success into your life in the fastest time possible. You can also benefit from taking calculated risks in the stock market and other legal forms of gambling, or from taking a chance on a new idea that just comes to you.

The purpose of life is to be happy. If you think that statement is not true, then what does that say about what you believe the purpose of life is? Pleasure is a wonderful experience, I am sure you would agree. It is the opposite of pain, another fact no one will deny. However, what most people do not realize is the many ways in which pain, other than physical pain, is actually a resistance to love.

It is incredible how many people in our workaholic society think that they are not entitled to enjoy themselves. There is a great fear that if you admit you are having a good time some nasty power is going to take it away from you. I am here to tell you that nothing could be farther from the truth. The more you learn how to run your life from a position of what you enjoy, the better will be both your life and the lives of those around you. You are not being selfish when you are enjoying yourself; you are fulfilling your divine purpose for being a human being. If you do not allow yourself to enjoy pleasure, you can only be telling yourself that you would prefer to live with pain.

6TH HOUSE

The Sixth House rules how things work — your job, employees, devices that work for you, and also how your body works. It has to do with what you put into your body and the state of your health, including the mind-body connection. This is the house that rules food, farming, planting seeds, acorns, cooking, physicians, dentists, exercise, and servants. While the Third House has to do with the relations between people, the Sixth House has to do with the different services people perform for each other, everything from manual labor to doing someone a favor. The negative aspect of the Sixth House is work done against your best interests, either by you or someone else. This is why traditional astrology assigned open enemies to this house. A more pleasant thing ruled by the Sixth House is small animals and pets.

Love/Relationships — *6th*

For the sake of your relationships, it is important that you, your partner, or both of you love your work or at least feel you are providing a useful service. If you do not, avoid bringing your work situation into your relationship because your complaints may produce problems. Now would be a good time for you to try working for the benefit of your partner, if your circumstances and your temperament are appropriate for such a daunting task.

A relationship with someone you work for or who works for you will become important now. If you are not in a relationship now, one might come to you either through your work, co-workers, or through any volunteer work that you do. Any relationships that come into your life now will have an element of service to them, either you helping your new friends or they you.

If you are healthy in mind, body, and spirit, you are more blessed than you can imagine. If you are not, it is important that your relationships are with people who understand your position and want to do all they can to help you cope with your challenge. Do not waste your time with people whose fears drive them away from people who need help. We are all healing from the challenges we have lived through and can share our experience and coping techniques with those who want our help. Remember, however, not to force your help on anyone.

Sometimes this card can indicate that you and your partner may becoming more aware of your habits regarding health, cleanliness, neatness, eating, sleeping, and working. Little habits that become known too soon might prove the undoing of a relationship. Once you have gotten to know, like, and respect each other's differences and similarities, these little habits are far more likely to be tolerated.

Work/Career — *6th*

This is the ultimate sign that you have to work hard. This is not the time for slowing down or retiring. Any job you recently thought was over will require you to work on it again in some way. If you are out of work, take the first job that comes your way. You will be able to make something out of almost any job. At this time, it is not what line of work you are in but how hard you work that counts.

Crucial to your career is your willingness to do the often boring, routine, and even menial tasks that need to be done. Expecting someone else to take care of them will only delay the kind of job you may desire. Get down to work and get your hands dirty now, even if it seems pointless. This is a time for you to be recognized for what you can do, not for what you say you can do. It is time to show those in a position to help you in some way that you are not afraid to work hard.

Working too hard would be just as bad as not working hard enough. In your attempt to balance your career goals with your physical and mental health, you must pay attention to what some people consider minor details — health habits, rest and relaxation, and proper nutrition. Those who ignore them because they are too busy working often come to regret it. Many people are willing to avoid taking proper care of their body's needs in their pursuit of a career. However, the hard work that you have to do now will pay off someday and then you will want to be as healthy as you can be in order to enjoy it to the full.

WEALTH/SUCCESS — *6th*

At this time, the best way for you to make money is the old fashioned way — to earn it. This is not a time when things will just be handed to you. Everything you get now will be the result of hard work you have done. If you do get money advanced to you for work that you have not done yet, be very careful with it. Your hard work is going to tire you and, unless you pace yourself, you may not have the stamina to complete what you start. Treat your health like the ultimate wealth that it is. Without it, no amount of material wealth and success is going to be as useful to you.

Worries about your lack of wealth and level of success will actually stop the flow of both things to you. No matter what your goal is, you have all that you need to get what you want. It is a matter of accepting your situation, starting from where you find yourself, and taking small but practical steps toward your goal.

How you are able to deal with life on a mental and emotional level determines how those things will manifest in your life. If you remember that you are strong and can handle anything life brings you, you will bring into your life experiences that will enable you to prove this is true.

If you have doubts about your abilities, life will bring you challenging circumstances designed to show you how strong you really are. Sometimes it takes overcoming fairly unpleasant circumstances to convince you of your intelligence, strength, and endurance. Maintain a positive, confident, and grateful attitude and you are truly wealthy and successful. Do not let what you lack prevent you from enjoying what you have. There is always someone worse off than you are.

7TH HOUSE

The Seventh House rules committed relationships of a romantic and business nature, not necessarily marriage, but definitely not casual relationships or fleeting romance. This is the house of divinely blessed soul mates or, at the very least, relationships that are destined to last for a long time. Seventh House relationships often involve oral and written contractually binding agreements between people obligating them to perform specific duties on specific dates and times. This is the house of rules and law, though not necessarily of justice. Court cases, lawsuits, and negotiations are all Seventh House matters. Contracts and business partnerships are often made public, and a marriage is the public declaration of love and lifelong partnership. For this reason, the Seventh House rules coming before the public and publicity. Scheduled parties and all social engagements of a formal nature that you are somehow obligated to attend are ruled by this house.

LOVE/RELATIONSHIPS — *7th*

Now is the time for your relationships to be perfected. If you are happy with things the way they are, then keep doing what you are doing and know that they are going to get even better. If you do not have a relationship but you would like to have one, drawing this card is the closest thing to a guarantee that you will soon have one. And it may be your soul mate. It is not something that you can look for; it sort of finds you. The way you can know if you have found your soul mate is if neither of you wants to change the other, only to enjoy life together and to help each other fulfill your individual dreams. This does not happen on the first date, but the basic feeling of mutual attraction, trust, respect, and friendship can be sensed if you are quiet and sensitive enough. Wishful thinking can easily confuse the issue, so relax and be yourself.

Any trouble in a relationship now will come from one or both of you not fulfilling your obligations with honesty and a giving heart. You or your partner may have learned from others whom you looked up to and respected that this unequal and disappointing way was the way to act in a relationship. Troubled marriages and divorce can affect the participants and their children a lot more than anyone would care to admit.

The trick in both romantic and business relationships is to avoid living your life through the needs and demands of your partner. That way, you will not have to acknowledge your own needs and take action to make your dreams come true. A relationship based on the satisfying of the needs of only one of the people involved is doomed to failure.

WORK/CAREER — *7th*

Do not try to go it alone now. You can advance your career more if you work in a partnership where you both clearly understand the parts you are playing in the arrangement and what it is you are working for.

Pay attention to the obligations you have at work. Fulfill your part of all agreements, rules and regulations. Find a way where you can work with others without feeling that you have to give up your unique personality.

If you are having problems at work, look honestly at how your actions are being interpreted. Though you may have had the best of intentions, at some point in the near or distant past, your actions may have created conflict. Think more before you act and consider others' feelings to be as important as your own. Even if you were being as nice as you could be, a misunderstood word, a look, or your tone of voice may have given the impression that you were not willing to be a team player. You may have gotten a reputation as someone who is bossy or difficult.

Whether you are looking for a new job or trying to do your best where you are, make a special effort not to appear too bossy. Nobody likes a know-it-all or someone who says, "I told you so," even if you did. Would you rather be right or do what's best for your career? Compromise is not cowardice.

This is not the time for you to be doing work that keeps you from interacting with the public or co-workers. Jobs that would work for you now could involve the law, contracts, working with the public, publicity, negotiations, and working in the support industries that service weddings and parties. If possible, your work should have you as an equal part of a team.

WEALTH/SUCCESS — *7th*

You will be luckier now if you join forces with a partner so as to take advantage of the benefits gained by two sets of connections, two chances to get lucky, and two people to help each other make decisions. Now is the time where it will benefit you to keep the advice of others in mind. Even if you feel the need to develop your self-reliance now, you will not be able to live in a world without other people. Your challenge is to be strong enough not to lose your individuality even though you have to be with another person to accumulate the wealth and success you have worked for. It is not anyone else's job to make you feel complete. But you will find that other people will be much more generous with you now.

All manner of contracts and legal matters are favored now. It would be a good time to bring a legal matter to the forefront of your activities. With the accent on luck from partnerships, you will be most likely to find the best person to represent you. Of course, the best people never mind when you check to make sure that they really are the best. So do your homework and you will have the peace of mind that comes from knowing you have done your due diligence.

Publicity and coming before the public in all manners are also favored. If you are called on to speak in public or deal with the public, you will do very well. Now is a time when other people want to help you, some because they believe that by helping you, they further their own cause. Now is a time when other people will be acting like agents operating on your behalf, or you may benefit from representing someone else.

H
O
U
S
E
S

8

8ᴛʜ House

The Eighth House rules the transmission and exchange of resources and other kinds of energy between you and others, and between you and the universe. The ability to share and transform other people's resources connects the Eighth House with magic, power, and the mysteries of life, especially sex. It is the house of extremes like good and evil, man and woman, and yin and yang. It also has to do with extremes of power — both the good that enables needed change to occur without harm and bad, such as crime, compulsions, and perversion. It is the house of other people's money — loans, money that you manage for other people, and inheritances. It also rules resurrection, rebirth, and transformation, including the ultimate transformation — death and the spirit. Remembering the reality of our death and the death of all we love is frightening, especially at first, but doing it as a spiritual practice keeps things in perspective and helps us appreciate the precious, fleeting, gift of life.

LOVE/RELATIONSHIPS — *8th*

Relationships now can have an element of sexual tension, mystery, magic, and possibly compulsion. If your relationship has lost its spark, it must be rekindled or it will surely die. If this is true for you now, the two of you must begin a slow, patient, and loving dialogue about how things have gotten to this point and how you are going to transform your relationship. You will have to use all of your detective skills to keep the transformation moving along, but you can do it.

If you do not have a relationship now, one is about to appear as if by magic. You will recognize it by the intensity of the feelings it produces in both of you. Be mysterious and keep your secrets. You can reveal them when you get to know each other better.

It will be very hard for you to resist giving yourself completely to this new love, but you should wait until you have proven your love to each other in other ways first. The reason people have sex before they are truly in love is because there is no training in what love and a loving relationship really is. A person who loves you for yourself should be understanding about any decisions you make, especially about something as important as sex. All too often, the sexual urge is not seen as just that, an urge. Blindly following our primal urges, whether they be to lust, violence, or other desires to work our will on others, can only lead to disaster.

Many people equate the desirability of a potential partner with the amount of uncontrollable or overwhelming desire they inspire. This is all well and good if it exists along with mutual respect and genuine caring. Growing old together should be viewed as a privilege to be desired.

H
O
U
S
E
S

WORK/CAREER — *8th*

If you have been thinking about making changes in your work situation or career, now is the time to make them. It could range from rearranging or moving your office all the way to changing jobs or changing careers altogether. This is a time of extremes, so be prepared for change to come and not necessarily from where you think it might come.

Keep secrets and do not volunteer any information. If you are thinking about a career change, hint to your most trusted work associates that you are thinking about whether or not to pursue a career change you abandoned long ago. If they are enthusiastic, you can tell them more. If they offer you their help, take it. Every successful person has received help from outside sources at one time or another and there is no reason to let foolish pride stand in the way of your new career.

It is time for you to learn how to use other people's money and resources to your advantage. If you have been working hard to obtain the trust of those with whom you work, it is time for you to ask for more responsibility in your job, including handling other people's money. If your request is granted, you must treat it as a sacred trust. Whether you work with money or not, it is crucial that you resist any and all enticements to use your power for your own gain. It would also be a good idea to make sure that your colleagues are being completely honest in their dealings with you and your place of work.

Now is a great time to work in banking, asset management, recycling, estate planning, detective work, the "mantic" arts (astrology, the tarot, magic, and the like), and in matters related to sex.

WEALTH/SUCCESS — *8th*

It is time to make magic. Now is a good time to transform your resources profoundly. It will take thorough research, absolute secrecy, and a healthy suspicion of other people, but it can be done. Investments of time, money, and other resources that you might have thought dead and buried can now come back to life in some mysterious way. You may find that something you tried and failed at is now the perfect thing to be able to profit from. Check your records and see what you have that you can now rework and transform profitably.

Once you know what to do, it would be better to use a majority of other people's resources rather than all of your own. If you have friends or family who might help you with a loan, grant, or early inheritance, now would be a good time to ask. If not, then investigate obtaining financial assistance from the many institutions, both governmental and private, which exist for just that purpose. Do this investigation in secret.

A financial grant or loan would give you the freedom to devote yourself full time to the realization of your dreams for wealth and success. You can now gain financial wisdom from your efforts to obtain and pay back your loans from banks and individuals. Once you have gotten your new enterprise going, your investments will prosper, and you may find yourself in the position of helping to guide the wise use of other people's money as an advisor.

This is also the perfect time to plan your estate. Nothing lasts forever, not even you, and it is important that you plan for the transformation of your resources after you leave this world. It is very important to make sure that your desires are carried out after you go. You might even think about becoming an organ donor.

H
O
U
S
E
S

9TH HOUSE

The Ninth House has to do with the transmission and exchange of important information between you and the world. One aspect of this is travel and everything that helps you travel — travel that broadens your understanding of the world, or that allows you to exchange ideas with many different people. Other ways to learn about the customs and beliefs of people that are not in your neighborhood are through reading books, newspapers, magazines, and electronically transmitted information of all kinds, like the Internet, television, radio, and other wireless communications devices. The communications ruled by the Ninth House are about sharing college level thinking, expert advice, historical facts,

H
O
U
S
E
S

philosophy, cultural anthropology, cartography, and research of all kinds. The Ninth House also has to do with justice, which is not the same thing as the laws of the Seventh House. Justice requires that you apply law with the wisdom and truth that the Ninth House rules. Justice should not be blind.

LOVE/RELATIONSHIPS — *9th*

If you cannot take a trip with your committed partner, then you should at least plan one and learn as much as you can about where you would like to go. Learning a foreign language would also be a good idea now. You would be surprised how romantic the incredible wisdom stored in a library can be when you have a good reason to be there.

If you do not have a relationship now, taking a trip or planning one as above may very well bring one to you. Learning a language and going to the library or other places to learn would also expose you to new ideas and people. You might even find yourself involved with someone who is not like you and your family, and might actually be from a different part of the world. Or a person might be involved in broadcasting, publishing, travel, philosophy, or research.

Problems you are now experiencing regarding your love life are the result of attitudes and experiences caused by people outside your relationship having too much influence on it. This may be manifesting as one of you giving the appearance that you are still under the control of a close friend or family member. This can cause problems because it gives the appearance that you or your partner is not special or smart enough to be considered as equally important as this close friend or family member.

This can also manifest itself as too much physical separation. One of you may be spending too much time away from the other, either at work, with friends, or with family. Or your sense of privacy may feel violated when you realize your partner is talking about your private affairs with others and acting on their advice, not on yours. No matter what the problem, take the high road and use the example of only the wisest people in the world to solve it.

WORK/CAREER — 9th

Remember that now is the time for you to break out of any boring routines. Your present job must provide you with the opportunity to expand your understanding of the world in some way. If it is possible for you to obtain any kind of on-the-job training, by all means do so. Going to school outside of work would also be very helpful. If you are unable to do work that interests you, increases your work skills, or furthers your education, it may be time to look for another job, without leaving your present one until you have the other job in hand.

Another way this might manifest itself is if you were able to travel overnight for your work, transfer to a distant location, or maybe even work in a foreign country. It is important to find out how people around the world approach your job or their equivalent of your job. You may find valuable help in advancing your career from incorporating the best ideas the world has to offer about your line of work.

Professions that would be good now would be travel, broadcasting, publishing, research, philosophy, education, motion pictures (especially documentaries), and writing books, as opposed to writing articles. Whatever you do now, it would be a good idea to approach it as a lifelong learning experience, rather than a job.

Interestingly, you may be called upon to teach others the valuable skills you already possess but may not value as highly as do others around you. If you are asked, do so. Your interaction with your students will end up teaching you many things. It will also remind you of what you may have known but forgotten. The polarity of learning and teaching is very important to your career right now and should be pursued at every opportunity.

WEALTH/SUCCESS — *9th*

In the near future, everyone else is going to think you are a lucky person. Of course, you will know that your coming good fortune is the result of your hard work encountering opportunities that you have worked for and deserve. But, to other people, you are going to be seen as possessing pure luck. Get used to this feeling. You are going to learn what it is to have other people think you have it all.

All manner of contests, awards, and prizes are favored, but especially the ones that expand your awareness or involve travel. Travel would benefit you more now that at most other times in your life, and you will probably find yourself traveling more than ever or dreaming about doing so. Indulge your wanderlust whenever possible. The money you spend will come back to you multiplied in opportunities for growth and expansion on many levels.

You will soon be hearing of a golden opportunity to broaden your mind. Even in your routine dealings with people, both at work and in your home, there is going to be a fantastic opportunity to learn or teach a wonderful new way of doing things.

Opportunities from far away are going to come to you. They are going to be in forms that are new and maybe a bit strange to you. You may have to overcome your natural reluctance to go out of your way and pursue all opportunities that come to you. The more foreign they are, the better. In fact, people born in countries or in cultures very different from your own are most likely to benefit you in some way. Their unique philosophy of life will expand your way of looking at things, and you will become aware of opportunities that you would have otherwise missed.

H
O
U
S
E
S

10

10TH HOUSE

The Tenth House is related to authority of all kinds. It represents how you experienced the dominant parent/caregiver in your home while you were growing up, the person who imposed structure, rules, and discipline on you. It also rules how you feel about those who have authority over you now, including how you think they feel about you, and how you feel about becoming an authority. Whether or not you respect yourself and how you value and respond to the respect of those you respect are Tenth House matters. We have used an Angel blowing a trumpet to symbolize the Tenth House because it is your calling in life. It is about founding your personal dynasty and creating your destiny and what will live on after you pass away in time. Achievement and everything that achievement requires and produces are Tenth House matters. Fame is another issue, your attitude toward fame and famous people, and your capacity for becoming famous.

Love/Relationships — 10th

Your relationships now must be able to withstand public scrutiny. You or your partner may become more widely known soon and your relationship may be held up as an example, for better or worse. If things are going well between you, then there is nothing to worry about. If your relationship has been going through hard times lately, now is the time to do what you can to try to make things better. Perhaps the drive to become recognized and the hard work and sacrifice of personal time have created the problems. If so, take a few days off to just be together with no plans or goals. This applies to love relationships and business relationships, too.

If you do not have a relationship now, one may soon come to you through your interactions with authority figures. You may meet someone through an authority figure or you may actually become involved with an authority figure of some stature. This could be anyone who is respected by you or more typically by a group of people. Another way this might be manifested is if you met someone while you were functioning as an authority figure, yourself, or working on becoming one. Or your next partner could just be famous or infamous.

You may find yourself attracted to a person who reminds you of the parent you most respected or were disciplined by. This could also manifest itself as an older person being your next partner. If you are in a relationship, then you may find yourself noticing how much your partner is actually like that same parent and it may come as quite a shock. Or it may be your partner who notices the resemblance. This is just pointing you to the next area of life that the two of you are going to be working on together.

WORK/CAREER — 10th

At this time, you are in an excellent position to advance your career and prestige. There is a good chance that you are going to be recognized and rewarded now. Fame can come your way more easily now than at other times. At some time in the near or distant past you demonstrated your ability to work well both alone and with others. You also made it perfectly clear that you could come up with innovative solutions to any questions and problems that came your way. You have made your way of doing things look easy, both to others and maybe even to yourself. However, at this time, it is necessary for you to take any and all necessary steps to get serious about your career.

You must get serious about where you find yourself right now. Where you are right now can provide you with all the resources you need to succeed, if you adopt a serious attitude towards your career. Even if you end up leaving what you are doing, you will be able to look back and realize that you accomplished your move with resources derived from where you are today.

If you find yourself between jobs, it is important that you present yourself to prospective employers as someone who has everything she needs to do the job. It is very important that you become employed in the near future so take the best of any jobs you see become available without delay. You are at the point where your steady climb to the top is beginning to be noticed by others. Work hard now and you will be able to enjoy yourself later. It is important that you look at the big picture now and avoid dwelling on little things that will slow you down.

WEALTH/SUCCESS — *10th*

It is time to reap the rewards of your long climb to the top. The expression "fame and fortune" sums up the picture for you now. First will come the kind of admiration that will be easy to call a kind of "fame," and then, how you deal with your fame will determine exactly how and when your fortune will be arriving. That will be a time when you will come to know exactly where you are going and how you are going to get there. However, before that time, you are most likely to first find yourself being congratulated and even elevated in status above where you are used to being. In fact, you may find yourself looked to for wise council or guidance. It is time for you to get to know what it feels like to be an authority figure.

At this time, you are in excellent position to gather all the recognition for your achievements that you so richly deserve. It is a time when you begin to realize your destiny. Those around you and especially those you look up to and wish to emulate will recognize you for the positive changes you are making and do all they can to help you. Your efforts will be acknowledged and supported in many ways.

The recognition you are about to receive may not bring you wealth immediately, but it will in the long run. Not only will it inspire you to keep up the good you are doing, but also any honors you receive will help you command a higher price for your services in the future. For the while, you will be concerned with putting together a structure for your future wealth, so that when it comes to you, you will know how to make the best of it.

11TH HOUSE

The Eleventh House has to do with groups of people you interact with because you share common goals and aspirations, or you can be more effective banding together to accomplish them. This can be your circle of friends, clubs, trade unions, organizations, political parties, fraternal organizations, team sports, sailing and rowing crews, volunteer fire and ambulance corps, charities, and social movements — local, national, or global in scope. What you hope or wish for is the essence of the Eleventh House. Taking action to make your dreams come true is as satisfying as having fun; in fact, one is essential for the other to happen. It is all the variations on the theme of invention. It is creativity with a purpose

HOUSES

that will benefit other people as much if not more than it will benefit you. The Eleventh House also rules the unexpected in all forms, a factor that must be considered in all forecasts of the future.

LOVE/RELATIONSHIPS — 11*th*

If your committed partner, lover, or business partner is also your friend, then you can expect things to get even better than they are. If your partner is not someone you think of as your friend, then try to change that now or you may be in for an unsettled time. All too often people will not be as kind, understanding, or forgiving to those they supposedly are in love with as they will be to their friends. If this is the situation in your relationship, you must either change things or you could eventually end up changing partners.

If you do not have a relationship, getting involved with groups of people who have come together for a common goal will help you find one. This can be through your circle of friends. It could also be through getting involved with people who are in fraternal organizations, societies, clubs, trade unions, trade associations, environmental groups, political activism, chat rooms, theme cruises, tour groups, group therapy and all other ways that people get together for mutual support. This is also a time when going to a place that exists to help people meet potential partners would be favored.

Though passion is important in a relationship, at this time it would be better if the two of you shared a passion for the attaining of a particular goal; it could be yours, your partner's, or a shared goal. Planning for the future is an important part of relationships for you now. If you are in one where the focus is on the past without using its lessons to plan your future, then you may have to see your dreams come true with another partner. The exception to this would be if you confronted your partner and he or she was able to look at the situation dispassionately, realize the truth of what you are saying, and take real steps to change that behavior.

H
O
U
S
E
S

WORK/CAREER — 11*th*

At this time, things have progressed to the point where readjustment is needed. You should be open to new ideas regarding your career. It is very important that you do not assume too much about how you make your living. Remember that each of us is extremely unique. We all know a different truth about life. It has even been said that each of us is a living example of a different truth about life. If you assume you know how things are going you will not be open to the new opportunities that are all around you at this time.

If you are set on the attainment of a career goal in one particular way to the exclusion of all other ways of attaining your goal, you must expect things to take far longer than they would if you allowed the unexpected enough room to work its magic. There is usually more than one path to reach the top of a mountain. You must look within your heart to see if your attachment to the method of attaining your goal is slowing you down or even preventing you from reaching that goal altogether. It is time to allow yourself to remove your nose from the grindstone so you can look up and see how the world around you has changed. The way you have been operating regarding your career was decided by you in the past. Things are different now and what was true for you then is no longer so. Get comfortable with change.

If you do not have work now or are thinking about changing careers, working for groups that have organized for a common goal would be favored. There are many variations on this theme, but some would be trade unions and associations, fraternal organizations, credit unions, Internet chat rooms and the like, political groups, environmental and other cause groups.

WEALTH/SUCCESS — 11*th*

At this time, your good fortune is more likely to come to you through your friends than through other ways. They may bring you good fortune in the form of a gift, advice that you can profit from, or they, themselves, may be the ones increasing their wealth and they will be happy to share it with you.

If you are disturbed by the prospect of accepting gifts and other help from your friends, you must look inside yourself and examine the standard you are holding yourself to. When did you first think that being helped was weakness? Where did this idea come from? Are you expecting yourself to be better than it is humanly possible to be? Are you the kind of person who likes to share good times with your friends? Then why not let them do it for you?

If you have ever sat around day dreaming with your closest friends, then those are the dreams most likely to come true. Those that treasure your friendship have remembered your hopes and wishes and may have come across a unique way to make your dreams a reality.

Friends from the past may re-enter your life. Though you may not want to welcome them with open arms or pick up just where you left off, it would be in your own best interests to spend time with them and see what they have been up to. Remember, you may have told them wishes you have long ago forgotten. It is good for you to be reminded of the things you used to wish for. You will be surprised to see how many of them you have gotten. Being aware of how far you have come will help you plan how to get where you want to be. Plan for your retirement now.

12TH HOUSE

The Twelfth House is associated with everything that helps you to remember that you are a small part of a great whole. The overwhelming beauties of nature, looking at a work of art, or entering a cathedral are perfect examples of this humbling but inspiring feeling. These things can make you feel extremely alone, sad, insignificant and needing to escape and, at the same time, in awe of the majesty and grandeur of life and its infinite beauty. Both the sorrow and the joy of life can bring us to tears. The Twelfth House also has a shy, hidden dimension of privacy to it, like the hour of the first light of dawn. It rules a person's innermost being, including the subconscious, intuitive, and psychic dimensions of her mind. It also rules secret enemies and large institutions like hospitals, corporations, government, organized religions, and the armed forces.

LOVE/RELATIONSHIPS — 12*th*

At this time, some kind of sacrifice will be required of you, your partner, or both of you for a purpose that is more than simply personal. One or both of you may be involved with a large institution at this time and needing help to deal with that situation. There may be events taking place that make it hard for one or both of you to feel strong enough to cope with the situation and therefore you must each do what must be done to support one another. If this mutual support is lacking at this time, then you should try and do what you can to get this problem out in the open and corrected. If there is no hope of that happening, then you may have to sacrifice your relationship or sacrifice your right to enjoy your life.

If you are without a partner now, finding one may be tricky. The element of sacrifice does not fit easily with the standard view of courtship and romance. However, the exception to this would be if you were dedicated to helping others or you, yourself needed help, and met someone because of that. If you were both on the helping end, this would be more prone to lasting than if one of you was helping the other person. This would not be a relationship founded on mutual support, so it might need substantial reworking if the person receiving help no longer needed it. Sometimes, relationships last only as long as the problems being worked on exist.

The early dawn might be when you start or strengthen your relationships. Getting involved with religion, charities, the government, corporations, or any other form of large institution would be a great way to improve your love life and your love of life.

H
O
U
S
E
S

Work/Career — 12*th*

Now is a time to go with the flow, not make waves, and put your own needs second to those of the common good. Any freely given sacrifice you might make now would work to your benefit later. However, doing so with the expectation of receiving benefit would substantially lessen any benefit that might come to you later. This is the time to be like a worker ant, not a queen bee.

It would benefit you to become involved in work and causes where you are a small part of a major effort. Working with large institutions such as the government, hospitals, the armed forces, large corporations, organized religions, global movements, or charitable causes would be very good for you. It is necessary for you to get to know how people less fortunate than you feel about life, but not just intellectually. You are going to have to feel what they feel to do the best job you are capable of. While you may find some of the things you learn about how other people live a bit shocking, the benefit to your career will be great.

If you were between jobs, applying for help at a large institution, especially one dedicated to helping others, would work out nicely now. Until your new job comes through, it would be highly beneficial for you to volunteer your services. Any experience you would gain as a volunteer would prove highly useful to your new job. In fact, a new and exciting career might come to you as a result of your volunteer work.

Whatever job you do, it is crucial that you plan to spend some time absolutely alone every day. You are going to be seeing and doing things that may make you want to escape, so escape into your own private world to lessen your stress level. Try meditation.

Wealth/Success — 12th

At this time, wealth and success for you will be determined by how much you are doing to help others, especially those less fortunate than you. Even if you do not have much to share, now would be a great time to give what you could.

Success through interactions with corporations and large institutions is very likely at this time. You are most likely to succeed in areas of life where you are just a small cog in a big machine, not focused on yourself but on helping to keep everything moving. The government, the military, museums, as well as hospitals, prisons, religions, and charitable organizations are very likely to bring you benefits. All of these organizations require people to sacrifice their desires for a higher purpose and that is precisely the attitude that would benefit you the most now.

At this time, your faith can move mountains. It is a time to let forces bigger than you work through you for your highest good and greatest joy. In fact, it would benefit you to ask for what forces outside yourself think you would benefit from receiving. You will be given help in proportion to the help you give others.

Very big contests where you are an anonymous entrant would work well. Raffles and other kinds of games where you were a number or other sort of nameless contestant would work out well. All contests and lotteries run by the government, museums, charitable organizations, and large corporations, as well as contests held to benefit those less fortunate would also be favored.

Giving selflessly requires that you take time every day to be by yourself to restore your energy and process what you are involved with. One thing to be aware of is—are you helping people who deserve your help?

H
O
U
S
E
S

ABOUT THE AUTHORS

*W*hen artist Amy Zerner met writer Monte Farber in 1974, an enchanted relationship was formed. Since that time the two have married and become the foremost designers of interactive divination systems in the world. Since 1988, Amy and Monte have created eleven divination systems for self-transformation and the development of intuition, three children's books, a coffee-table art book, an album of music, and a CD-ROM series, which they refer to collectively as "spiritual power tools." There are over one million copies of their books in print in nine languages.

*A*my Zerner is the first and only artist working primarily in fabric to win a major National Endowment for the Arts fellowship grant in the category of Painting. Her unique talent as an image-maker results in art that is based on inner visions, dreams, myths, and fairy tales. Her work combines textiles, embroideries, papers, and assorted found objects to create visionary images intended to act as signposts to spiritual growth and healing.

*M*onte Farber distills the results of decades of studying astrology, the tarot, mythology, philosophy, and many other forms of ancient and modern wisdom into a form easily understood by today's audience. In addition to being a writer, Monte is an inventor, musician, businessman, agent, teacher, motivational speaker, seminar leader, and, of course, interpreter of Amy's art.

*I*n all their work, the power of Amy's incredibly beautiful fabric collage tapestries are combined with Monte's words to create a unique and sacred synergy that heals, inspires, and empowers. In their work and their workshops, they share with their audience the kindness, good humor, and deep wisdom that has enabled them to find love, spirituality, contentment and genuine success in their enchanted lives.

Continue your journey through *The Enchanted World of Amy Zerner and Monte Farber*. Like *The Enchanted Astrologer*, the following award-winning divination systems are also beautiful intuition-building tools for self-discovery; share them with a special friend, use them to make your parties sparkle, and savor them in moments of private reflection:

The Instant Tarot Reader
St. Martin's Press, ISBN: 0-312-16681-8

The Enchanted Tarot
St. Martin's Press, ISBN: 0-312-05079-8

The Oracle of The Goddess
St. Martin's Press, ISBN: 0-312-19179-0

The Psychic Circle
Simon & Schuster, ISBN: 0-671-86645-1

The Pathfinder
Tuttle Publishing, ISBN: 1-885203-89-6

Gifts of The Goddess
Chronicle Books ISBN: 0-8118-2729-1

Karma Cards
Penguin Books, ISBN: 0-14-015487-6

The Enchanted Tarot CD-ROM
Enteractive, ISBN: 1-887233-05-9

The Alchemist CD-ROM
Enteractive, ISBN: 1-887233-02-4

PRINTS & POSTERS

Prints and posters of many of Amy Zerner's more than 600 collages and fabric tapestries, including reproductions of all of the Signs of the Zodiac images from your Enchanted Astrologer deck, can be obtained on paper or canvas by calling toll free 888-376-7600 or by E-mailing orders@buyenlarge.com.

*T*o receive a color catalog describing the full line of products from *The Enchanted World of Amy Zerner and Monte Farber*, or to be notified of their upcoming appearances, workshops, cruises, and the exhibitions of the art of Amy Zerner, please call 1-800-308-3578 or write to:

The Enchanted Astrologer
Zerner/Farber Editions, Ltd.
Post Office Box 2299
East Hampton, NY 11937, USA

If you have access to the Internet, please visit our enchanted website:
http://www.TheEnchantedWorld.com

You can also e-mail us at:
info@TheEnchantedWorld.com

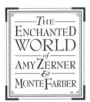